Understanding Freshwater Gamefish

MINNETONKA, MINNESOTA

Author Dick Sternberg combines his fisheries biologist background with his multi-species angling talents to produce a book that will not only help you understand every important kind of freshwater gamefish, but help you catch them as well.

Understanding Freshwater Gamefish

Mike Vail
Vice President,
Products and Business Development

Tom Carpenter
Director of Book and New Media Development

Dan Kennedy
Book Production Manager

Jenya Prosmitsky, Dave Schelitzche
Book Design & Production

Gina Germ
Photo Editor

Michele Teigen
Book Development Coordinator

Bruce Holt
Proofreading

Photography
Bill Lindner Photography (Bill Lindner, Tom Heck, Mike Hehner, Jason Lund, Pete Kozad)
Dick Sternberg
Chris Batin
Denver Bryan
Tom Carpenter
Joe Daniel
Mark Emery
Kevin Erb
Dan Gapen
C. Boyd Pfeifer
Doug Stamm
Gillbert Van Ryckevorsel
Bill Vanderford
Don Wirth

Illustration
Duane Raver, Jr., p. 102
Maynard Reece, pp. 90, 128, 130 both, 136, 141, 146, 152, 154
Dave Schelitzche, pp. 13, 52, 70, 71, 75, 91, 145
Joe Tomelleri, pp. 7,10, 12, 14 both, 16, 18, 21, 24, 26, 28, 30, 32, 34, 36, 41, 44, 46, 51, 54, 58, 63, 66, 69, 72, 74, 76, 78, 82, 85 both, 88, 94, 96, 98, 102, 107, 109, 111, 112, 117 all, 118 both, 120, 123 both, 124,126, 133, 138, 141, 142, 146, 148, 150
Jon Q. Wright, pp. 136, 144, 146

9 8 7 6 5 4 3 2 1

ISBN 1-58159-037-7

North American Fishing Club
12301 Whitewater Drive
Minnetonka, MN 55343

Contents

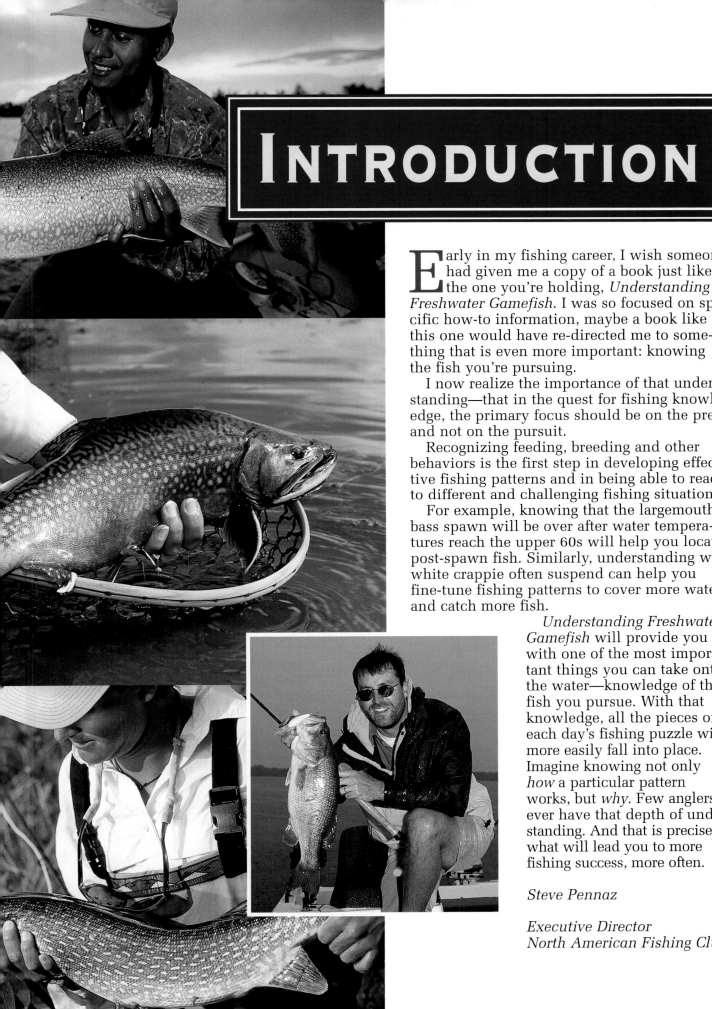

INTRODUCTION

Early in my fishing career, I wish someone had given me a copy of a book just like the one you're holding, *Understanding Freshwater Gamefish*. I was so focused on specific how-to information, maybe a book like this one would have re-directed me to something that is even more important: knowing the fish you're pursuing.

I now realize the importance of that understanding—that in the quest for fishing knowledge, the primary focus should be on the prey and not on the pursuit.

Recognizing feeding, breeding and other behaviors is the first step in developing effective fishing patterns and in being able to react to different and challenging fishing situations.

For example, knowing that the largemouth bass spawn will be over after water temperatures reach the upper 60s will help you locate post-spawn fish. Similarly, understanding why white crappie often suspend can help you fine-tune fishing patterns to cover more water and catch more fish.

Understanding Freshwater Gamefish will provide you with one of the most important things you can take onto the water—knowledge of the fish you pursue. With that knowledge, all the pieces of each day's fishing puzzle will more easily fall into place. Imagine knowing not only *how* a particular pattern works, but *why*. Few anglers ever have that depth of understanding. And that is precisely what will lead you to more fishing success, more often.

Steve Pennaz

Executive Director
North American Fishing Club

SUNFISH FAMILY

This large and diverse family includes many of our most popular game-fish species. It is comprised primarily of 3 major fish groups: sunfish (genus *Lepomis*), crappies (genus *Pomoxis*) and black bass (genus *Micropterus*). Altogether, the family includes 32 species in the United States and Canada, 15 of which are popular enough among anglers to be included in this book.

All members of the sunfish family are warmwater fish. They thrive in shallow lakes, shallow portions of deeper lakes, ponds, slow-moving streams and river backwaters.

The family name, *Centrarchidae*, means "nest builders." Prior to spawning, the male of the species sweeps out a nest with his tail. The female moves in, the pair spawn, and then the male stays on to guard the eggs until they hatch and the fry are large enough to leave the nest.

Although this parental care ensures good survival of the young, it also leads to a problem that is common among many of the family's smaller members. When too many of the young fish survive, they compete with each other for food and living space and often become stunted.

LARGEMOUTH BASS

(Micropterus salmoides)

Varieties

There are two subspecies of largemouth bass: the northern largemouth (*Micropterus salmoides salmoides*) and the Florida largemouth (*Micropterus salmoides floridanus*). They look nearly identical, the only difference being that the scales are a little smaller on the Florida bass. The latter, which were originally found only in the Florida Peninsula, grow much faster and reach a considerably larger size than northern bass, with several 20-plus pounders on record. The giant bass currently being caught in California and Texas are Florida largemouths.

Habitat

Largemouth bass are found in all of the lower 48 states and their range extends into southern Canada, Mexico and Cuba.

Largemouth inhabit weedy natural lakes, reservoirs with plenty of woody cover, sluggish streams and small ponds or pits with adequate depth. They can tolerate water clarity ranging from only a few inches to 20 feet or more. They are more salt-tolerant than most freshwater fish, which explains why they are found in tidewater rivers. The largemouth's preferred temperature range is 68 to 78°F.

Feeding Habits

Largemouth may well be the least-selective feeders of all freshwater fish. The bulk of their diet includes a variety of small fish (including their own young), crayfish and larval aquatic insects. But they also eat small mammals, salamanders, frogs, worms, leeches, snails, turtles and even small snakes. When the water dips below 50°F, however, largemouth do very little feeding.

Spawning Behavior

When the water warms to the lower 60s in spring, male largemouth move into the shallows to begin building their nests. They normally nest in a bay or along a shoreline that is sheltered from the wind, usually around weedy or woody cover. Using his tail, the male fans away silt to reach a firm sandy or gravelly bottom, then the female moves in to deposit her eggs.

Largemouth bass range.

• *Also called bigmouth, bucketmouth, black bass, linesides.*

Largemouth bass are greenish to tannish in color with a darker back, lighter belly and a dark horizontal band. The jaw is longer than that of the smallmouth, extending past the rear of the eye.

A big Florida bass.

Typical Growth Rates

| Age | Northern Largemouth | | Florida Largemouth | |
	Length (inches)	Weight (pounds)	Length (inches)	Weight (pounds)
1	4.8	—	5.9	—
2	8.7	0.3	12.8	1.5
3	11.1	0.8	15.7	2.8
4	13.6	1.7	17.6	4.2
5	15.5	2.4	20.4	6.4
6	17.4	3.2	22.1	8.3
7	18.3	3.7	23.1	9.6
8	19.4	4.9	23.4	10.1
9	20.2	5.6	24.8	12.2
10	21.0	6.2	25.6	13.3

By the time the water reaches the upper 60s, most spawning is completed. The male guards the nest and stays with the fry until they disperse.

Age/Growth

Largemouth have been known to live as long as 16 years, but it is unusual for them to live for more than 10. Although the growth rate of Florida bass far exceeds that of northern bass, Floridas stocked in the North grow no faster than the native bass.

An 8-year-old northern largemouth typically weighs about 5 pounds; a Florida of the same age but in the South, about 10 pounds.

World Record

22 pounds, 4 ounces; Montgomery Lake, Georgia; June 2, 1932.

Where to Find Largemouth Bass

Natural lakes with medium to high fertility and an abundance of weedy cover hold dense populations of largemouth bass.

Man-made lakes of moderate depth, especially those with plenty of flooded timber and submerged brush, make ideal largemouth habitat.

Fishing Facts

Largemouth bite best when water temperatures are in the 60s and 70s. They're most active under dim-light conditions. On bright, sunny days, they usually tuck into dense cover, where it's difficult to get a lure to them.

Because of their non-selective feeding habits, largemouth will eagerly attack practically any kind of artificial lure or live bait. Even so, a good largemouth fisherman must be versatile. There are times when the fish want topwaters and times when they want deep-running baits. Another important consideration is the type of cover. In heavy weeds, for instance, you need a bait that won't foul or hang up. On a clean bottom, you're better off with a bait that has open hooks.

Plastic worms and other soft-plastic baits can be "Texas-rigged" (with the hook point buried, top) for fishing in heavy cover or "Carolina-rigged" (with the hook point exposed, bottom) for fishing on a clean bottom.

A spinnerbait is a good choice for catching largemouths in heavy cover. You can toss it into weedy or brushy cover and not worry about it hanging up or fouling, because the spinner shaft acts as a weedguard for the upturned single hook.

When you're trying to locate bass, tie on a crankbait. You can cover a lot of water in a hurry, and largemouth find the enticing wiggle hard to resist.

When largemouth are finicky, try "finesse fishing" by using a super-slow presentation with a small bait. Rig a 3- or 4-inch soft plastic on a plain hook with only a split shot for weight and then inch it along the bottom.

SMALLMOUTH BASS
(Micropterus dolomieui)

• *Also called bronzeback, black bass, Oswego bass.*

Smallmouth are greenish to bronze in color, accounting for their common name, "bronzeback." They have dark vertical bars or diamond patterns on their sides, but these marks are not always present and may come and go. The cheek also has dark bars. The jaw extends to approximately the middle of the eye, which is often reddish. Neosho smallmouth have a black spot on the rear margin of the gill cover.

Varieties

There are two recognized subspecies of smallmouth bass. The northern smallmouth (*Micropterus dolomieui dolomieui*) is, by far, the most common. The Neosho smallmouth (*Micropterus dolomieui velox*) has been nearly wiped out by construction of dams on its native streams in Oklahoma, Arkansas and Missouri.

Habitat

Smallmouth are found in most types of natural lakes and reservoirs, and in rivers and streams with moderate current. They rarely inhabit small ponds, shallow lakes, sluggish streams or any muddy or badly polluted water. They prefer a hard bottom, usually rock or gravel, and are seldom found on a soft, mucky bottom.

Although smallmouth are considered warmwater fish, they lean slightly toward the coolwater category. They prefer water in the 67 to 71°F range.

Feeding Habits

Smallmouth are especially fond of crayfish, but they also eat a variety of other foods including frogs, insect larvae, adult insects and many kinds of minnows and other small fish.

Feeding slows considerably when the water temperature drops below 50°F.

Spawning Behavior

Spawning takes place in spring, usually at water temperatures in the mid 60s. The

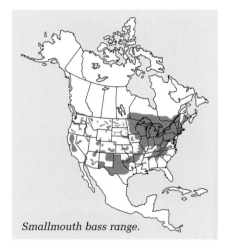

Smallmouth bass range.

male selects a spawning site on a sand-gravel or rock bottom in a protected area, often next to a boulder or log. He fans the silt from the bottom with his tail, then the female moves in to deposit her eggs.

After spawning is completed, the male stays on the nest to guard the eggs and, later, the fry.

Age/Growth

In the North, smallmouth bass may live as long as 18 years. They rarely live half that long in the South, but they grow considerably faster.

In northern waters it takes about 8 years for a smallmouth to reach 3 pounds, but in the South, only 4 years.

World Record

10 pounds, 14 ounces; Dale Hollow Lake, Tennessee; April 24, 1969.

Typical Growth Rate

Age	Length (inches)	Weight (pounds)
1	5.0	—
2	8.7	0.3
3	11.1	0.8
4	13.7	1.4
5	15.8	2.5
6	17.5	3.5
7	18.4	4.0
8	19.2	4.7

Fishing Facts

Many would argue that smallmouth are the strongest-fighting freshwater gamefish. Smallmouth prefer smaller food items than largemouth, explaining why anglers generally use smaller baits.

Smallmouth lures, such as jigs and crankbaits, are often intended to mimic crayfish in both action and color. Smallmouth will hit other kinds of lures as well, including minnowbaits, in-line spinners, spinnerbaits and topwaters.

Natural-colored lures, such as this jig and smoke grub, are usually a better choice for smallmouth than gaudy lures.

Any lure or fly that mimics a crayfish is a good choice for smallmouth bass.

SPOTTED BASS

(Micropterus punctulatus)

• *Also called spot, Kentucky bass.*

Spotted bass have light greenish sides with a dark lateral band consisting of irregular blotches. The jaw is shorter than that of a largemouth, but longer than that of a smallmouth, extending nearly to the rear of the eye. Each scale below the lateral band may have a distinct dark spot. Spotted bass have a small patch of teeth on their tongue (below). The northern spotted bass (shown above) has a distinct dark spot at the base of the tail, a vague spot on the gill cover and 60 to 68 scales along the lateral line.

Varieties

There are two existing subspecies: the northern spotted bass (*Micropterus punctulatus punctulatus*), by far the most common, and the Alabama spotted bass (*Micropterus punctulatus henshalli*). The Alabama subspecies—found in Mississippi, Georgia and Alabama—differs from the northern spotted bass; the dark spot on the Alabama

bass's gill cover is more distinct and there are more scales (68-75) along the lateral line. Another subspecies, the Wichita spotted bass, is probably extinct.

Spotted bass have been known to hybridize with smallmouth bass.

Habitat

Spotted bass inhabit deep, rocky, clearwater reservoirs and clear streams with fairly slow current. Their preferred temperature range is 73 to 77°F. They are normally found in deeper water than largemouth or smallmouth, usually in areas with little weed growth.

Feeding Habits

Like smallmouth bass, spots feed heavily on cray-

Spotted bass range.

fish. But they also eat small fish, including shad, and immature aquatic insects.

Spawning Behavior

Spotted bass usually spawn a little later than largemouth and about the same time as smallmouth. Most spawning activity takes place at water temperatures from 63 to 68°F. The male makes a nest on a rocky or gravelly bottom (usually at a depth of 4 to 20 feet) near a log, boulder or brush pile. After spawning is completed, he guards the nest until the eggs hatch and the fry disperse.

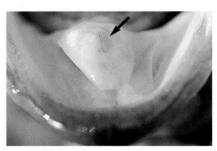

A distinguishing feature of the spot is the tiny patch of teeth on the tongue (arrow).

Typical Growth Rate

Age	Length (inches)	Weight (pounds)
1	7.3	—
2	11.0	0.7
3	12.2	0.9
4	13.9	1.3
5	15.4	1.7
6	17.1	2.3
7	18.3	2.9

Age/Growth

The life span of a spotted bass is considerably shorter than that of a largemouth or smallmouth, and their growth rate is much slower. Spots rarely live longer than 7 years or reach a weight of more than 4 pounds.

World Record

9 pounds, 9 ounces; Pine Flat Lake, California; October 12, 1996.

Fishing Facts

The best time to catch spots is in spring, when they're patrolling the shallows. Cast a small spinnerbait or minnowbait along shorelines where you see spawning activity. Once spots go deep in summer, finding them is much more difficult. You may have to fish at depths of 40 to 60 feet. Although spots seldom reach the size of largemouth or smallmouth, they're normally caught in snag-free water, so you can get by with fairly light tackle.

Look for spotted bass along steep, rocky ledges in clear man-made lakes. The ledges hold good numbers of crayfish, the spot's favorite food.

In summer, spots commonly suspend over deep water to feed on schools of shad. Rig up a tailspin (inset), cast it out and count it down to the depth of the shad before starting your retrieve.

REDEYE BASS

(Micropterus coosae)

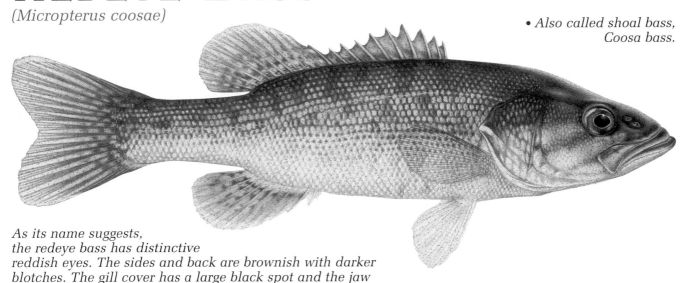

• Also called shoal bass,
  Coosa bass.

*As its name suggests,
the redeye bass has distinctive
reddish eyes. The sides and back are brownish with darker
blotches. The gill cover has a large black spot and the jaw
extends nearly to the rear of the eye. The Coosa bass (shown) has
reddish rear fins and blue spots on the back and sides. The belly may
be bluish as well.*

Varieties

Although the taxonomy of the redeye bass is continually being debated, most experts recognize two distinct forms: the more common Coosa bass, which is found in small streams in Alabama, Georgia, North Carolina and Tennessee; and the shoal bass, which lives in the Apalachicola river drainage in Florida, Georgia and Alabama.

Habitat

Redeyes prefer water temperatures in the mid 60s, below the range favored by other black bass. Coosa bass often inhabit the cool headwaters of small streams; shoal bass are usually found in larger rivers and streams.

Feeding Habits

Insects, both terrestrial and aquatic, are an important food for redeye bass. They also eat crayfish and small fish.

Redeye bass range.

Spawning Behavior

In spring, when the water temperature reaches the low to mid 60s, male redeyes begin making nests on gravel beds, usually at the head of a pool. Males protect the nest until the fry leave.

Age/Growth

Coosa bass grow very slowly and seldom reach a weight of more than 1 pound. Shoal bass grow much faster, at about the same rate as smallmouth (p. 11). Redeyes may live up to 10 years.

Shoal bass have a dark spot at the base of the tail, but they lack the reddish fins and bluish coloration of the Alabama redeye.

World Record

Coosa Bass: 8 pounds, 3 ounces; Flint River, Georgia; October 23, 1977.

Typical Growth Rate

(Coosa bass)

Age	Length (inches)	Weight (pounds)
1	1.9	—
2	3.2	—
3	4.3	—
4	5.5	—
5	6.6	0.1
6	7.6	0.2
8	8.4	0.3
10	10.1	0.5

Fishing Facts

Catching Coosa bass may be a challenge. They often hide under tree roots, logs and other overhead cover where it may be difficult to place a bait. The best strategy is to let the current drift an unweighted worm, minnow, crayfish or hellgrammite into their hiding spot. Coosa bass will also strike tiny spinners, nymphs, poppers and other topwaters. The techniques used for shoal bass are similar to those used for largemouth or smallmouth.

Redeyes, particularly Coosa bass, are often found around boulders or other cover that offers heavy shade.

Look for Coosa bass in the headwaters of small streams. You'll often find them in water that looks better suited to trout than to bass.

BLACK CRAPPIE

(Pomoxis nigromaculatus)

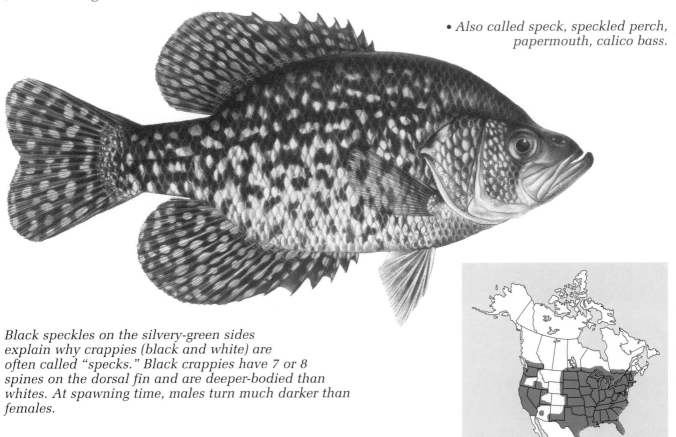

• *Also called speck, speckled perch, papermouth, calico bass.*

Black speckles on the silvery-green sides explain why crappies (black and white) are often called "specks." Black crappies have 7 or 8 spines on the dorsal fin and are deeper-bodied than whites. At spawning time, males turn much darker than females.

Black crappie range.

Varieties

Black crappies occasionally hybridize with white crappies.

Habitat

Clear, weedy natural and man-made lakes make ideal habitat for black crappies. They also inhabit backwaters and slow-moving reaches of warmwater rivers and streams. Black crappies prefer clearer, deeper, cooler water than white crappies, favoring water temperatures in the low 70s.

Feeding Habits

Important foods include small fish, immature aquatic insects and zooplankton. In summer, black crappies spend a good deal of their time foraging for zooplankton suspended over open-water

areas of lakes. Black crappies feed most heavily early and late in the day and at night. Feeding continues through the winter.

Spawning Behavior

Black crappies are spring spawners. Males begin making nests at water temperatures in the low 60s, often in brushy cover or in stands of emergent vegetation remaining from the previous year. Nests are often in colonies, with as many as 30 nests in a 100-square-foot area. After spawning has been completed, the male guards the nest until the fry disperse.

Age/Growth

The maximum life span of a black crappie is 10 years. On the average, it takes about 7 years for a black crappie to reach 1 pound.

World Record

6 pounds; Westwego Canal, Louisiana; November 28, 1969.

Typical Growth Rate

Age	Length (inches)	Weight (pounds)
1	3.0	—
2	6.1	—
3	8.2	0.3
4	9.3	0.5
5	10.2	0.7
6	11.1	0.8
7	12.1	1.0
8	12.7	1.3
9	13.2	1.6

Fishing Facts

Black crappies are easiest to catch in spring, when they move into shallow bays and channels to feed. Fishing is also good during the spawning period, when you'll find the fish in emergent weeds or brushy cover.

Although minnows are the number-one bait, black crappies will also strike small spinners, jigs and crankbaits. Fly fishermen have good success on wet flies and ice anglers catch good numbers of blacks on jigging lures.

Look for black crappies in shallow, mud-bottomed bays in early spring. These waters warm earliest, attracting baitfish which, in turn, draw crappies.

A slip-bobber rig baited with a small minnow hooked through the back probably accounts for more crappies than any other rig or artificial lure.

WHITE CRAPPIE

(Pomoxis annularis)

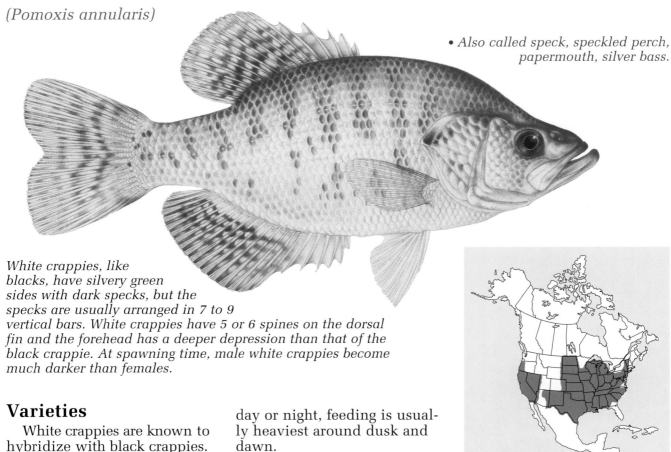

• Also called speck, speckled perch, papermouth, silver bass.

White crappies, like blacks, have silvery green sides with dark specks, but the specks are usually arranged in 7 to 9 vertical bars. White crappies have 5 or 6 spines on the dorsal fin and the forehead has a deeper depression than that of the black crappie. At spawning time, male white crappies become much darker than females.

Varieties

White crappies are known to hybridize with black crappies.

Habitat

White crappies and black crappies sometimes share the same lakes, streams and river backwaters, but whites can tolerate murkier water. They also prefer slightly warmer water temperatures, from the low to mid 70s.

Feeding Habits

Like black crappies, whites commonly feed on suspended zooplankton, explaining why they often suspend over open water. They also eat immature aquatic insects and small fish. In many southern reservoirs, threadfin shad are the major food for white crappies.

Although white crappies may feed at any time of the day or night, feeding is usually heaviest around dusk and dawn.

Spawning Behavior

Spawning takes place in spring, normally at water temperatures in the low 60s. The male builds a nest on a firm to slightly soft bottom, usually under tree roots or overhanging banks in 1 to 5 feet of water. Nests are usually in tight colonies, like those of black crappies. After spawning, males guard the nests until the fry swim away.

Age/Growth

Although white crappies grow more rapidly than blacks, they don't live as long. A white crappie's maximum life span is about 8 years.

White crappie range.

Typical Growth Rate

Age	Length (inches)	Weight (pounds)
1	4.7	–
2	6.6	0.2
3	8.5	0.4
4	9.9	0.6
5	11.3	0.8
6	12.1	1.0
7	13.0	1.3
8	14.2	1.8

World Record

5 pounds, 3 ounces; Enid Dam, Mississippi; July 31, 1957.

Fishing Facts

White crappies are cooperative biters but weak fighters. They're easiest to catch in spring when they move into the shallows to spawn, but you'll have to work heavy cover to locate them. In summer, you'll often find the fish suspended in open water. You can catch white crappies on the same baits and lures used for blacks (p. 17).

During the spawning period, drop a minnow into openings between the branches of fallen trees or brush piles. The fish nest in colonies, so when you get a bite, work the area thoroughly.

When white crappies are in weedy or brushy cover, use a spin-rig (a small, skirtless spinnerbait), tipped with a minnow.

Understanding Freshwater Gamefish

BLUEGILL

(Lepomis macrochirus)

• *Also called bream, copperbelly, sun perch, sunfish, sunny.*

Bluegills have a light blue edge on the gill cover. The "ear" is pure black and there is a black blotch at the rear of the dorsal fin. The sides are brownish gold with a purple sheen and have a series of vague vertical bars. The breast of the male (shown) is copper colored.

Bluegill range.

Varieties

Bluegills commonly hybridize with pumpkinseed, green, redear, redbreast and longear sunfish. They may even cross with rock bass and warmouth. In some waters, hybridization is so common that it's difficult to know what you're catching.

There are two distinct subspecies: the northern bluegill (*Lepomis macrochirus macrochirus*) and the Florida bluegill (*Lepomis macrochirus mystacalis*).

Habitat

Practically all warm, shallow, weedy waters support bluegills. They abound in small, shallow lakes, in protected bays of larger lakes and in slow-moving reaches or backwater areas of rivers and streams. They prefer water temperatures in the mid to upper 70s.

Feeding Habits

Bluegills feed mainly on small crustaceans and molluscs, plankton, fish fry and aquatic insects. They eat

Female bluegills have a yellowish rather than copper-colored breast, and their overall coloration is lighter than that of the male.

Florida bluegill range.

guards the nest until the fry disperse.

The bluegill's reproductive potential is extremely high, with a single female sometimes depositing more than 200,000 eggs. Spawning may occur at monthly intervals over the summer, usually around the full moon. Unless there is enough predation to thin the bluegill crop, stunting is likely. As a result, waters with low bluegill populations generally produce the largest fish.

Age/Growth

Bluegills may live up to 10 years, but their usual life span is 5 years or less. Their growth rate is highly variable, depending mainly on population density.

World Record

4 pounds, 12 ounces; Ketona Lake, Alabama; April 9, 1950.

The Florida bluegill has a bluish back and lighter sides with about 7 distinct vertical bars. At spawning time, the male develops a copper-colored patch above the eye, accounting for the common name "copperhead."

more larval insects than adults, although there are times when they take large numbers of adult insects off the surface.

Spawning Behavior

Bluegills spawn in spring, when the water temperature reaches the upper 60s. The male selects a spawning site, usually at a depth of 3 feet or less, on a sandy or gravelly bottom protected from the wind. He sweeps away the silt with his tail, making a light-colored depression. After the female deposits her eggs, the male aggressively

Typical Growth Rate

Age	Length (inches)	Weight (pounds)
1	4.1	—
2	5.2	—
3	6.2	0.2
4	7.1	0.4
5	7.9	0.5
6	8.5	0.6
7	8.9	0.7
8	9.3	0.8
9	9.7	0.9

Fishing Facts

Catching bluegills is easy; they abound in practically any body of water suited to largemouth bass. The challenge comes in catching big ones. A body of water that has good-sized bluegills often draws hordes of anglers, and the fish are soon removed.

Although the majority of bluegills are caught on live bait—particularly worms, leeches, grubs and crickets—they can also be taken on tiny artificials such as jigs and spinnerbaits. They will rise to small poppers, sponge bugs and dry flies.

When you hook a bluegill on light tackle, it gives you a good tussle for its size. But there is another important reason for the species' tremendous popularity—they're tops on the dinner table, with firm, white, flaky, sweet-tasting meat.

Use a long cane pole or extension pole for fishing bluegills in emergent weeds. This way you can place your bait in a small pocket without casting and then lift the fish straight up so it doesn't wrap around the vegetation.

Bluegills are more surface-oriented than other sunfish. When they're in shallow water, you can easily take them using a small popper.

Tiny jigs in the ^{1}/64-to ^{1}/32-ounce range rank among the top bluegill lures. You can fish them plain or tip them with a small piece of worm or other live bait.

After spawning, bluegills usually move to deep water. Use your depth finder to locate the fish and then try still-fishing with live bait on a slip-bobber rig.

PUMPKINSEED

(Lepomis gibbosus)

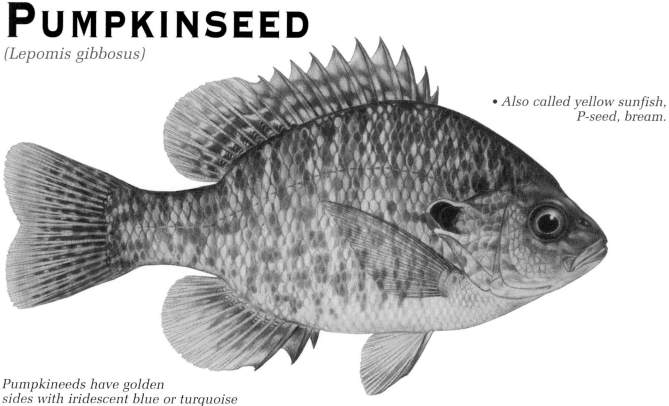

• *Also called yellow sunfish, P-seed, bream.*

Pumpkineeds have golden sides with iridescent blue or turquoise mottling and numerous red or orange flecks. The upper half of the body has 7 to 10 dark vertical bars, which are more noticeable on females. The cheeks are streaked with blue and there is a reddish spot at the tip of the "ear."

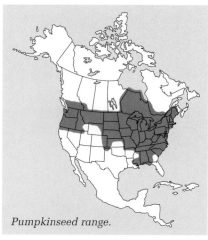

Pumpkinseed range.

Varieties

Pumpkinseeds often hybridize with bluegills and sometimes with green, longear, redear and redbreast sunfish. They have also been known to cross with warmouth.

Habitat

Normally found in shallower, weedier water than bluegills or redears, pumpkinseeds are most common in small lakes and protected bays of larger lakes. They also inhabit weedy backwaters and slow-moving stretches of warmwater rivers and streams. They prefer water temperatures in the low to mid 70s, cooler than that favored by most other sunfish species. This explains why their range extends as far north as Hudson Bay.

Feeding Habits

Insects, both aquatic and terrestrial, comprise the bulk of the diet, but pumpkinseeds also feed heavily on snails and may eat small crustaceans and fish fry.

Spawning Behavior

Spawning takes place in late spring at water temperatures in the upper 60s. Pumpkinseeds normally spawn earlier than bluegills and in shallower water. The male makes a nest on a firm bottom, usually among emergent plants in water less than 2 feet deep. After spawning is completed, he closely guards the nest until the fry are ready to abandon it.

Age/Growth

Pumpkinseeds grow slowly and seldom reach a weight of more than ½ pound during a full 10-year life span. Males have a slightly faster growth rate than females. And even though the current world record is from South

Carolina, pumpkineeds in the northern part of the range generally grow faster and reach a larger size than those in the southern part.

World Record

2 pounds, 4 ounces; North Saluda River, South Carolina; May 26, 1997.

Typical Growth Rate

Age	Length (inches)	Weight (pounds)
1	1.4	—
2	2.6	—
3	4.0	—
4	5.2	0.2
5	6.7	0.3
6	8.0	0.5
7	9.1	0.7

Fishing Facts

Because of their tiny mouths, pumpkinseeds are notorious nibblers, so it's important to use small baits and tiny hooks—no larger than size 8. Favorite live baits include worms, leeches and grubs; artificials such as small spinners and curlytail grubs are also effective. Fly fishermen rely mainly on tiny poppers, nymphs and wet flies. Pumpkinseeds do not fight as well as bluegills, but they are equally tasty.

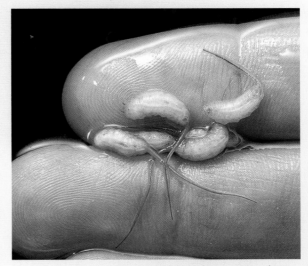

Tiny larval baits, like "mousies" (shown) or "waxies" (waxworms), are ideal because they easily fit into the pumpkinseed's small mouth.

Toss a worm and small float into a pocket in the weeds. Jiggle the float a little and then pause for a few seconds. If you don't get a bite, reel up and cast to another pocket.

REDEAR SUNFISH
(Lepomis microlophus)

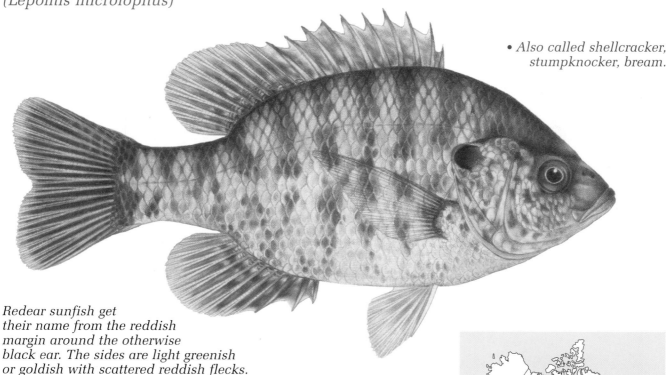

• *Also called shellcracker, stumpknocker, bream.*

Redear sunfish get their name from the reddish margin around the otherwise black ear. The sides are light greenish or goldish with scattered reddish flecks.

Varieties

Hybridization with bluegill, longear, pumpkinseed and green sunfish is fairly common.

Habitat

Redears normally inhabit clear lakes with moderate weed growth. They are seldom found in current, but may live in river backwaters. They prefer water temperatures in the mid 70s. Redears are more tolerant of brackish water than other kinds of sunfish.

Feeding Habits

Redears seldom feed on the surface; they commonly pick up invertebrates, particularly small snails and clams, off the bottom, explaining why they're called shellcrackers. They also eat immature aquatic insects and fish eggs.

Spawning Behavior

Redears spawn in late spring or early summer, usually at water temperatures from the upper 60s to about 70°F. The male constructs a nest on a firm bottom, often along the edge of submergent or emergent vegetation. After spawning is completed, the male guards the eggs and fry until they are ready to leave the nest.

Age/Growth

Compared to other sunfish, redears grow rapidly, commonly reaching weights in excess of 1 pound. They live up to 8 years.

World Record

5 pounds, 7 ounces; Diversion Canal, South Carolina; November 6, 1998.

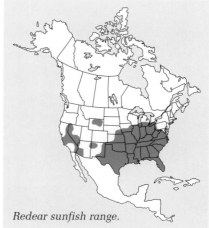

Redear sunfish range.

Typical Growth Rate

Age	Length (inches)	Weight (pounds)
1	4.9	—
2	7.0	0.3
3	8.1	0.5
4	9.1	0.7
5	9.8	0.9
6	10.5	1.1
7	11.2	1.3

Fishing Facts

Redears are not as easy to catch as most other sunfish. They are less inclined to take artificials, but they can be caught on a variety of live baits including earthworms, catalpa worms, grass shrimp, crickets and grubs.

The majority of redears are caught during the spawning period. They may be hard to find once they leave the spawning beds and move to deeper water, but anglers who know where the shell beds are can usually catch fish.

Grass shrimp are one of the top shellcracker baits. You can buy the small crustaceans at many bait shops or find your own by picking through clumps of hyacinth.

Locate shell beds by poking the bottom with a long pole. When you feel the shells crunch, anchor up and start fishing.

LONGEAR SUNFISH

(Lepomis megalotis)

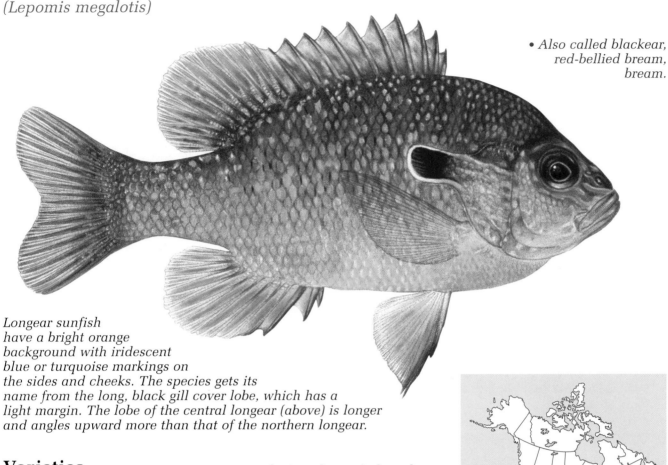

• *Also called blackear, red-bellied bream, bream.*

Longear sunfish have a bright orange background with iridescent blue or turquoise markings on the sides and cheeks. The species gets its name from the long, black gill cover lobe, which has a light margin. The lobe of the central longear (above) is longer and angles upward more than that of the northern longear.

Varieties

There are two subspecies: the central longear sunfish (*Lepomis megalotis megalotis*), which is the most common, and the northern longear sunfish (*Lepomis megalotis peltastes*), found only in the southern Great Lakes region.

Longears may hybridize with pumpkinseed, bluegill, redear and green sunfish.

Habitat

Like redbreast sunfish, longears thrive in moving water. They are most numerous in clear, gravelly streams with slow current, but they also inhabit lakes, ponds and reservoirs. They prefer water temperatures in the upper 70s to low 80s.

Feeding Habits

The diet consists mainly of insects, small crayfish, scuds, snails, fish eggs and fish fry.

Central longears (shown) resemble northern longears, but the gill cover lobe is longer. A northern longear is shown on p. 29.

Longear sunfish range.

They feed most heavily during the day, but may take insects off the surface on moonlit nights.

Spawning Behavior

Longears spawn in summer at water temperatures in the low 70s. The male makes a nest on a gravelly bottom, often in close proximity to other nests. After spawning is completed, he aggressively defends the nest until the fry have left.

Age/Growth

The maximum life span of a longear is 9 years. Central longears may reach a length of 9 inches; northern longears, only 5.

World Record

1 pound, 12 ounces; Elephant Butte Lake, New Mexico; May 9, 1985.

Typical Growth Rate

(CENTRAL LONGEAR)

Age	Length (inches)	Weight (pounds)
1	1.4	–
2	3.2	–
3	4.7	–
4	5.4	0.15
5	6.5	0.25
6	7.0	0.35

Fishing Facts

Most of these small sunfish are caught incidentally by anglers seeking other species. They are quite popular, however, in waters where they reach a decent size.

Longears are usually caught on worms, small minnows, crickets, grasshoppers or crayfish. Tiny spinners also work well, as do wet flies and nymphs.

Marinas on southern reservoirs often hold good-sized longears. Anglers commonly catch them off boat docks.

REDBREAST SUNFISH

(Lepomis auritus)

• *Also called yellowbelly sunfish, robin, bream.*

The redbreast gets its name from the male's reddish-orange breast, which becomes especially intense at spawning time. On females, however, the breast is more yellowish. The greenish sides have red-orange flecks and the cheek has bluish streaks. The black lobe on the gill cover is very long but, unlike that of a longear sunfish, does not have a light margin.

Varieties

Redbreast sunfish may hybridize with bluegill, pumpkinseed and green sunfish as well as warmouth.

Habitat

Primarily a moving-water species, redbreast sunfish inhabit rivers and streams along the Atlantic and Gulf coasts. They can tolerate a moderate salt content, but they're seldom found as far into the brackish water zone as are redears (p. 26). Redbreasts are sometimes found in lakes, particularly those connected to coastal streams. They prefer water temperatures in the low 80s.

Feeding Habits

Like most other sunfish, redbreasts feed mainly on immature insects, small crustaceans and fish fry. But they are more likely to feed at night than are other sunfish. Redbreasts do most of their feeding near the bottom, but will also take food off the surface. Feeding comes to a halt once the water temperature drops below 40°F.

Spawning Behavior

Redbreasts spawn in late spring or early summer at water temperatures in the upper 60s to low 70s. The male makes a nest on a firm bottom in water less than 2

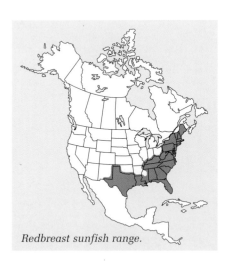

Redbreast sunfish range.

feet deep, usually near woody cover. He protects the nest until the fry swim away.

Age/Growth

Redbreasts rarely live longer than 6 years or reach a weight of more than ½ pound.

At spawning time, the male's breast develops an intense red coloration.

World Record

2 pounds, 1 ounce; Suwannee River, Florida; April 29, 1988.

Typical Growth Rate

Age	Length (inches)	Weight (pounds)
1	1.9	—
2	3.3	—
3	4.7	0.1
4	6.2	0.2
5	7.3	0.3
6	8.1	0.4

Fishing Facts

What redbreast sunfish lack in size they make up for in beauty. The male, with his flaming red breast, is the most colorful fish that swims in fresh water. Redbreasts have white, flaky meat that has an exceptionally sweet flavor.

Tough fighters for their size, redbreasts will take most of the usual sunfish baits, but they're especially fond of crickets and grasshoppers. They will also strike tiny spinners, fly-rod poppers, wet flies and sponge bugs.

Look for redbreasts around inlet streams and culverts. The fish are drawn to the moving water, which carries in insects and other foods.

Bait up with a cricket or hopper on a long-shank Aberdeen hook. Thread the insect on so the hook comes out the rear of the abdomen or just behind the collar.

GREEN SUNFISH

(Lepomis cyanellus)

• *Also called blue-spotted sunfish, rubbertail, bream.*

Green sunfish have light greenish to brownish sides shading to darker green on the back. The sides have iridescent bluish flecks, accounting for the common name "blue-spotted sunfish," and the cheeks have bluish streaks. Compared to most other sunfish, the mouth is larger and the body more elongated.

What green sunfish lack in size they make up for in aggressiveness.

Green sunfish range.

Varieties

Green sunfish may hybridize with bluegill, redear, pumpkinseed, longear and redbreast sunfish.

Habitat

Of all the common sunfish species, the green sunfish is most tolerant of muddy water, silty bottoms and low dissolved oxygen levels. Greens are commonly found in weedy lakes and ponds, and they sometimes thrive in muddy, sluggish creeks. Green sunfish prefer water temperatures in the low 80s, and they are usually associated with weedy, brushy or rocky cover.

Feeding Habits

Although the majority of their diet consists of insects and small fish, green sunfish have a relatively large mouth and are capable of eating surprisingly large food items. Green sunfish commonly eat crayfish, and researchers have found small carp and even bats in their stomachs.

Spawning Behavior

Green sunfish spawn in late spring or early summer at water temperatures in the upper 60s to low 70s. Males make nests, often in large colonies, on a firm bottom in water less than 2 feet deep. After spawning, they aggressively defend the nest.

Age/Growth

Green sunfish are short-lived, seldom reaching an age of more than 6. They are prone to stunting, and rarely reach a weight of more than ½ pound.

World Record

2 pounds, 2 ounces; Stockton Lake, Missouri; June 18, 1971.

Typical Growth Rate

Age	Length (inches)	Weight (pounds)
1	3.8	—
2	6.0	0.2
3	7.3	0.3
4	7.9	0.4
5	8.9	0.5

Fishing Facts

Although anglers seldom target these small sunfish, greens are caught incidentally while fishing for bluegills or other kinds of sunfish. In waters where they are not stunted, however, greens are worthy of an angler's attention. They are scrappy fighters and their white, flaky meat makes excellent eating.

Muddy, slow-moving streams sometimes have the best green sunfish fishing. In this type of habitat, the fish seldom become numerous enough that stunting is a problem.

Look for green sunfish in dense, woody cover that provides overhead protection and shelter from the current. Use a long pole and lower your bait vertically into small pockets.

ROCK BASS

(Ambloplites rupestris)

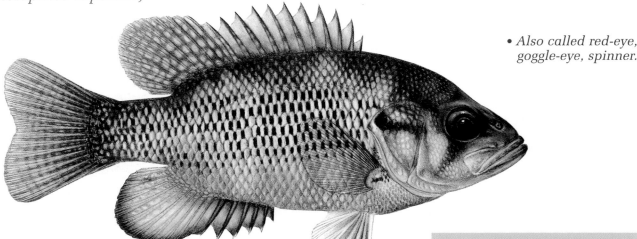

• *Also called red-eye, goggle-eye, spinner.*

Rock bass have brownish to goldish sides with rows of dark spots and dark blotches along the back. The reddish eye accounts for the common name "red-eye." Rock bass resemble warmouth, but the anal fin has 6 spines instead of 3. During the spawning period, male rock bass become much darker than females. The rock bass has been called "the chameleon of the sunfish family" because of its ability to change color to match its surroundings.

Varieties

Rock bass sometimes hybridize with a closely related species called shadow bass, and with warmouth and bluegill.

Habitat

The latin name of the rock bass, *rupestris*, means living among rocks. The fish do, in fact, inhabit rocky bottoms in clear, weedy lakes and slow streams. They prefer water temperatures in the upper 60s to low 70s.

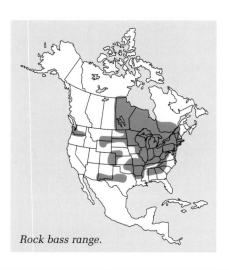

Rock bass range.

Feeding Habits

Small fish and crayfish make up the bulk of their diet in most waters, but rock bass also eat insects, clams and snails. They feed most heavily during daylight hours. Unlike most sunfish, rock bass feed very little during the winter.

Spawning Behavior

In late spring or early summer, when the water temperature reaches the upper 60s, the males begin making nests on a firm bottom, often in or at the edge of emergent vegetation such as bulrushes. The nests are usually in water less than 3 feet deep. After spawning has been completed, the male protects the eggs and fry.

Age/Growth

Rock bass have a maximum life span of about 13 years, longer than that of most sunfish. They commonly reach weights of 1 pound, but seldom exceed 1½.

World Record

3 pounds; York River, Ontario; August 1, 1974.

Typical Growth Rate

Age	Length (inches)	Weight (pounds)
1	1.6	—
2	3.0	—
3	4.5	—
4	5.9	0.2
5	7.1	0.3
6	8.3	0.5
7	9.1	0.6
8	9.6	0.7
9	10.1	0.8
10	10.5	0.9

Understanding Freshwater Gamefish

Fishing Facts

Rock bass are aggressive biters, eagerly attacking a variety of live baits and artificial lures. But they're held in low esteem by many fishermen because they are often infested with parasites, particularly yellow grubs.

Another reason for their lack of popularity: They put up a relatively weak fight on hook and line. In fact, some anglers call them "spinners" because they tend to spin around in circles as they are being reeled in.

Rocky, slow-moving warmwater streams, especially those with lots of crayfish, make ideal habitat for rock bass.

Hellgrammites (dobson fly larvae) are a favorite bait among stream fishermen. Simply hook the bait under the collar and weight it with a split shot or two.

WARMOUTH
(Lepomis gulosus)

• *Also called goggle-eye, stumpknocker.*

With its reddish eye and golden-brown sides with dark mottling, the warmouth closely resembles the rock bass. But it has several dark streaks radiating from the eye, it lacks the horizontal rows of dark spots and the anal fin has only 3 spines instead of 6.

Varieties

Warmouth sometimes hybridize with rock bass, bluegill, pumpkinseed, green sunfish and redbreast sunfish.

Habitat

Shallow, weedy lakes and ponds, slow-moving reaches of streams and river backwaters make the best warmouth habitat. The fish are often found on a muddy or silty bottom with plenty of woody cover. Warmouth prefer water temperatures in the low to mid 80s and can withstand temperatures into the low 90s.

Feeding Habits

Because of their large mouth, warmouth eat more fish than other kind of sunfish. Warmouth also feed on immature and adult insects, crayfish and snails.

Spawning Behavior

Spawning takes place in late spring or early summer, at water temperatures in the upper 60s. The male builds a nest in water from a few inches to 4 feet deep. Nests may be on a soft bottom, as long as there are stumps or weed clumps for cover. Males defend the nest until the fry are ready to leave.

Age/Growth

The maximum life span of the warmouth is about 8 years. Weights of more than 1 pound are unusual.

Warmouth range.

Typical Growth Rate

Age	Length (inches)	Weight (pounds)
1	3.3	–
2	5.2	–
3	6.1	0.3
4	7.3	0.4
5	8.3	0.5
6	10.0	0.9
7	10.8	1.1

World Record

2 pounds, 7 ounces; Yellow River, Florida; October 19, 1985.

Fishing Facts

You can catch warmouth using the same baits and techniques that you would for bluegills. A worm or minnow beneath a float probably accounts for most warmouth, but the fish are quite surface-oriented and will readily take small fly-rod poppers. They can also be caught on small wet flies and nymphs.

At spawning time, look for warmouth around stump fields in river backwaters. The fish may nest on the exposed tree roots.

Drop your bait into small openings in matted weeds. Set your float to fish only about 12 to 18 inches deep, because warmouth often lie right beneath the vegetation.

PERCH FAMILY

The perch family (*Percidae)* includes 130 species in the United States and Canada, but only 3 (walleye, sauger and yellow perch) are popular among anglers. The rest (darters and logperch) are too small to be caught on hook and line, and often serve as forage for the larger members of the family.

Percids are coolwater fish, meaning that they prefer water temperatures cooler than warmwater fish such as sunfish, and warmer than coldwater fish such as trout and salmon. They need a prolonged period of cold water for their eggs to develop properly, explaining why they do not occur naturally in the Deep South.

Unlike sunfish and trout, percids do not build nests. Instead, they scatter their eggs on the bottom and then abandon them. Survival of the fry is low in lakes with large numbers of sunfish or other small predators.

Walleye, sauger and yellow perch thrive in large natural and man-made lakes as well as big rivers. Saugers are the most current-oriented of the three; perch, the least. Originally, these fish were not found west of the Rockies, but extensive stocking has established them throughout the West and in most southern states.

WALLEYE

(Stizostedion vitreum)

• *Also called walleyed pike, pickerel and dore.*

Walleyes have golden sides and a white belly. The spiny dorsal fin is not spotted, but has a black blotch at the rear base. The lower lobe of the tail has a large white tip.

Walleye range.

Varieties

Walleyes sometimes cross with sauger, producing the saugeye (p. 45), which is intermediate in both looks and behavior.

Habitat

Walleyes thrive in large natural and man-made lakes and big warmwater rivers, but they're also found in a variety of smaller lakes and streams. Walleyes prefer a clean, firm bottom and water temperatures in the 65 to 75°F range. Surprisingly, they reach their highest abundance in waters of low to moderate clarity.

Feeding Habits

The bulk of an adult walleye's diet consists of fish, but walleyes also eat aquatic insects, various worms and leeches, crayfish, frogs and immature salamanders. In low-clarity waters, walleyes feed most heavily in midday; in clear waters, early and late in the day or at night.

Under dim-light conditions, walleyes have a predatory advantage over most baitfish because the retina of their eye has a layer of reflec-

The tapetum gives the walleye excellent dim-light vision.

tive pigment called the tapetum lucidum. The tapetum explains why the eyes of a walleye glow when struck by light.

Spawning Behavior

Spawning takes place in spring, usually at water temperatures in the upper 40s. The eggs are deposited along shallow gravel-rubble shorelines that are exposed to the wind. Walleyes are random spawners; they do not protect their eggs or fry.

Age/Growth

Although walleyes have been known to live more than 25 years, their normal life span is 7 or 8. Walleyes generally grow much faster in the South than in the North, but in some northern waters with good forage crops, walleyes grow nearly as fast as those in the South. Females normally grow considerably faster and reach much larger sizes than males.

World Record

22 pounds, 11 ounces; Greer's Ferry Lake, Arkansas; March 14, 1982.

Typical Growth Rate

Age	Length (inches)	Weight (pounds)
1	5.1	—
2	9.0	0.4
3	12.3	0.8
4	15.1	1.2
5	17.3	1.7
6	19.2	2.2
7	21.4	3.1
8	23.1	3.8
9	25.5	5.4
10	27.2	7.1
11	29.0	9.0

Al Nelson with his 22-pound, 11-ounce world-record walleye.

Prime Walleye Waters

Large mesotrophic lakes with sand-gravel shorelines are top walleye producers. Most of these lakes have an abundance of yellow perch for forage, and windswept shorelines that are ideal for walleye spawning.

Large warmwater rivers, such as the Mississippi and Missouri, support excellent walleye populations. The fertile waters teem with baitfish such as shad or smelt, and the varied habitat provides the necessary spawning and rearing areas.

Fishing Facts

Walleyes are strong but not spectacular fighters. They generally wage a dogged battle in deep water. As a rule, fishing is best during dim-light periods—around dusk or dawn, at night, or in cloudy weather. Walleyes bite especially well just before a thunderstorm, when the light level is rapidly falling. Walleyes take a variety of live baits including leeches, night-crawlers and minnows, but they can also be caught on artificials such as minnowbaits, crankbaits, jigs and spinners.

In clear lakes, try casting minnowbaits onto shallow reefs and shoals after dark. Walleyes in these lakes don't feed much during the day but, at night, they patrol the shallows in search of baitfish.

In big rivers, look for walleyes off the tips of current-brushed points. These spots make good feeding areas because they attract huge schools of shiners and other minnows.

Look for a mudline caused by waves crashing into a rocky shoreline or point. Plankton pushed in by the wind draws baitfish and the reduced water clarity allows walleyes to feed in comfort.

Lead-head jigs with bucktail, feather or soft-plastic dressing make excellent walleye lures. Jigs imitate minnows, the walleye's favorite food, and they are easy to keep on the bottom where walleyes spend most of their time.

SAUGER
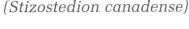

(Stizostedion canadense)

• *Also called sand pike, gray pike, spotfin pike.*

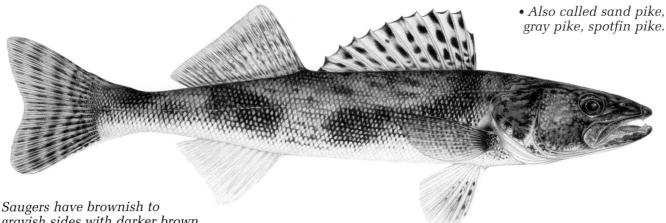

Saugers have brownish to grayish sides with darker brown "saddle" marks. The front dorsal fin has several evenly spaced rows of dark spots, and there is a dark spot at the base of the pectoral fin. The lower edge of the tail may have a thin, white band, but there is no distinct white spot as on the walleye.

Varieties

The saugeye (opposite) is a naturally occurring sauger-walleye hybrid.

Habitat

Saugers are fish of big rivers. Although they will tolerate stronger current than walleyes, they are typically found in slow-moving water.

Lakes fed by large rivers may support both saugers and walleyes. As a rule, saugers predominate in the upper reaches, where muddy river water keeps the clarity low. Walleyes are more numerous in the lower reaches, because the silt has had a chance to settle out and the water is clearer.

Saugers are often referred to as "sand pike," a name that reflects their preference for a sandy bottom.

Because the sauger's eye has an even larger tapetum lucidum than that of the walleye (p. 41), it can see even better than the walleye in dim light. This explains why saugers invariably inhabit deeper water than walleyes and why they commonly thrive in murky water.

The sauger favors water temperatures from the low 60s to the low 70s, but its location depends more on food source than water temperature.

Feeding Habits

Like walleyes, saugers feed primarily on fish. They also eat leeches, crayfish and a variety of immature aquatic insects. Because of their superb dim-light vision, they commonly feed at night and can easily find food in deep or discolored water.

Spawning Behavior

In most waters, saugers begin to spawn about the time walleyes are finishing. Walleyes usually start spawning at about 48°F; saugers, about 52. Walleyes deposit

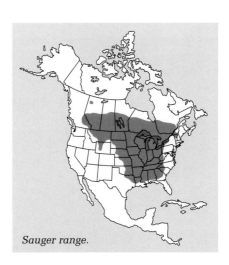

Sauger range.

their eggs in 1 to 6 feet of water; saugers, 4 to 12 feet. Although both species may spawn on the same rocky shoals, usually at night, the timing and depth preferences are different enough that there is little overlap.

Age/Growth

Although saugers may live up to 13 years, they generally have a shorter life span than walleyes. In most waters, their growth rate is much slower.

World Record

8 pounds, 12 ounces; Lake Sakakawea, North Dakota; October 6, 1971.

Typical Growth Rate

Age	Length (inches)	Weight (pounds)
1	5.8	—
2	9.4	0.3
3	12.6	0.7
4	14.6	1.1
5	16.3	1.5
6	17.6	1.9
7	18.4	2.2
8	19.1	2.5

Saugeyes (walleye/sauger hybrids) can be easily distinguished from saugers or walleyes by their front dorsal fin. It does not have the black blotch at the base, like that of a walleye, nor the rows of evenly spaced spots, like that of a sauger. Instead, it is mottled. **World Record Saugeye:** *15 pounds, 10 ounces; Fort Peck Reservoir, Montana; January 11, 1995.*

Fishing Facts

Although the maximum size of saugers is less than half that of walleyes, they are highly desirable game fish. They have white flaky meat much like that of a walleye.

But catching saugers can be tricky, especially in cold water. They have a frustrating habit of sucking on the bait without swal-lowing it. If you're using a minnow, it will often come back with a ripped up tail. The solution is to use a "stinger" hook.

Look for saugers on a sandy or sand-gravel bottom, usually where there is light current.

To catch short-striking saugers, use a jig and minnow with a stinger hook.

YELLOW PERCH

(Perca flavescens)

• *Also called raccoon perch, ringed perch.*

Yellow perch have bright yellowish sides with 6 to 9 dark bars. The lower fins often have an orange tinge and, on spawning males, are bright orange.

Habitat

Good-sized lakes with moderate depth, clarity and weed growth produce the largest yellow perch. The fish are most numerous in open-water areas with a firm bottom. Perch are also found in smaller lakes and ponds, and in warmwater streams with medium to slow current. They have been stocked extensively in the South.

Yellow perch are considered coolwater fish and prefer water temperatures from the mid 60s to low 70s.

Feeding Habits

Yellow perch are daytime feeders. The majority of their diet consists of immature aquatic insects and small fish, but they also eat fish eggs, crayfish, scuds, small clams and snails. Perch do most of their feeding near the bottom and commonly root in the mud for the larvae of mayflies and other insects.

Spawning Behavior

Yellow perch start to spawn shortly after ice-out, usually at water temperatures in the mid 40s. After dark, they drape long gelatinous strands of eggs over weeds, fallen branches or debris in shallow water. The parents do not guard the eggs or young.

Age/Growth

Although yellow perch may live up to 10 years, their normal life span is 6 years or less. Their growth rate varies considerably, depending mainly on the predator-prey balance. In many waters, perch are so numerous that they become stunted and

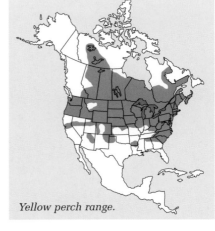

Yellow perch range.

Typical Growth Rate

Age	Length (inches)	Weight (pounds)
1	3.1	—
2	5.1	—
3	6.9	0.2
4	8.5	0.3
5	9.6	0.4
6	10.4	0.6
7	11.1	0.8
8	11.6	0.9
9	12.0	1.1

rarely reach a length of more than 6 inches.

Lakes that produce "jumbo" perch (those weighing ¾ pound or more) usually have a large population of walleyes, northern pike or other predator fish to keep the perch population thinned out.

World Record

4 pounds, 3 ounces; Delaware River, New Jersey; 1865.

Fishing Facts

Willing biters, yellow perch can be caught on a variety of live baits including worms, leeches, small minnows, waxworms, crickets and even tiny crayfish. Small jigs and spinners are also good producers.

Some of the biggest perch are taken by ice fishermen using jigging lures. The fish generally bite best in late winter as they begin to feed heavily in preparation for spawning in early spring.

Fertile lakes with heavy populations of scuds, or "freshwater shrimp," produce some of the biggest perch. The fish gorge themselves on the tiny crustaceans, which are only about ¹/₂ inch long.

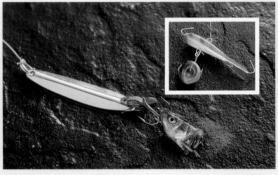

A jigging spoon or swimming minnow (inset) tipped with a minnow head or perch eye (where legal) is one of the most effective ice-fishing lures.

PIKE FAMILY

This family of toothy predators has only 5 members in the United States and Canada. The muskellunge, which is the largest member of the pike family (*Esocidae*), is considered by many to be North America's premier sport fish. The northern pike, one of the most widely distributed gamefish in the world, grows almost as large as the muskie, but the chain pickerel is considerably smaller. The other 2 species—grass and redfin pickerel—are too small to be of much interest to anglers.

All esocids have a long, slender body, a duckbill-shaped snout, a single dorsal fin near the tail and long, sharp teeth that can instantly shear monofilament line. Esocids are considered coolwater fish, explaining the northerly distribution of pike and muskie. But pickerel can tolerate warmer water temperatures and are found as far south as Florida.

Esocids are random spawners, not nest builders. In spring, they scatter their eggs in shallow, weedy areas and then abandon them. Soon after hatching, the largest fry begin to cannibalize the smallest ones.

The habit of eating large food items continues through life. It is not unusual for a full-grown pike or muskie to attack another fish from $1/3$ to $1/2$ its own length. This explains why anglers commonly use very large lures and baits.

NORTHERN PIKE

(Esox lucius)

• *Also called great northern pike, jack, snake, gator.*

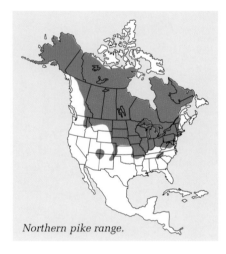

Northern pike range.

Northern pike have dark greenish sides with rows of oval-shaped, cream-colored marks. The fins usually have dark blotches and a reddish tinge.

Varieties

A mutant form of the northern pike, called the silver pike, occurs throughout the pike's range. Northern pike and muskies are often crossed to produce the tiger muskie (p. 55). Northerns have also been known to hybridize with chain and redfin pickerel.

Habitat

Pike are found in just about every conceivable type of water, from warm, shallow ponds to deep, cold lakes. They also thrive in most types of rivers and streams. But pike prefer lakes and streams that offer a coldwater refuge—a place where they can go in summer to escape the heat. Although most anglers believe that pike spend the majority of their time in shallow, weedy cover, the truth is that big pike often patrol deep water, where there is very little cover of any kind.

Biologists classify the northern pike as a coolwater fish. Small pike (those up to 30 inches long) prefer water temperatures in the 67 to 72°F range. But big pike favor much colder water. Given a choice, they will seek out water in the 50 to 55°F range. When forced to live in water too warm, pike grow very little and have a short life span.

The pike's ability to adapt to such a wide variety of habitat is reflected in its circumpolar distribution. In North America, their range extends from 40 to 70°N, encompassing most of the northern states and nearly all of Canada. Some of the world's best big-pike waters are in Europe and Siberia.

Silver pike have silvery, metallic-blue or greenish sides without the typical light, oval-shaped markings.

Feeding Habits

Pike eat just about anything that will fit into their mouth, but fish make up the majority of their diet. They prefer baitfish about 1/3 their own length and may even attack bigger fish. It's not uncommon to see a pike swimming around with the tail of a large fish sticking out its mouth. It gradually digests the prey over several days.

Pike are primarily sight feeders and are most active during daylight hours. They generally feed most heavily in overcast weather or when the water is choppy. Pike are less affected by the passage of a cold front than are most other gamefish.

Spawning Behavior

Northern pike spawn in early spring, soon after ice-out. When the water reaches 40 to 45°F, they swim up small tributary streams and deposit their eggs in adjoining marshes. If there are no suitable marshy areas, they will spawn in weedy bays. They do not build a nest, but scatter their eggs at random.

Age/Growth

Where pike have access to cool water, they are long-lived. In the Far North, pike have been known to live up to 25 years. Where they are forced to live in warmer water, however, they "burn out" rapidly, seldom living more than 6 years. Female pike live longer, grow faster and reach considerably larger sizes than males.

Records

World Record: 55 pounds, 1 ounce; Lake of Greefern, West Germany; October 16, 1986.

North American Record: 46 pounds, 2 ounces; Sacandaga Reservoir, New York; September 15, 1940.

Typical Growth Rate

Age	Length (inches)	Weight (pounds)
1	7.8	0.3
2	13.2	0.9
3	17.7	1.5
4	21.1	2.3
5	24.2	3.2
6	26.8	4.6
7	29.0	6.1
8	31.1	7.1
9	33.3	8.2
10	35.1	9.8
11	37.7	12.0

Other ID Features

A pike's entire cheek and the top of the gill cover are scaled.

The underside of a pike's lower jaw usually has 10 pores.

Where to Find Northern Pike

Weedy bays of natural lakes and weedy river backwaters are ideal for early-season pike. But as these waters warm in summer, the bigger pike move deeper to find cooler water.

In summer, look for pike on weedy humps (arrow) adjacent to deep water. Humps with plenty of broad-leaved cabbage (inset) are pike favorites.

Fishing Facts

A voracious predator, the northern pike will strike just about anything you toss into the water, but it's hard to beat flashy baits like spoons and large spinners. Other top producers include jerkbaits, jigs and crankbaits. And fly fishermen are discovering that big, bushy streamers and divers can be very effective.

Live bait—chiefly big suckers— also work well on pike (see below).

There's no need for a subtle presentation in pike fishing. Most anglers use heavy line (12- to 30-pound test) along with a heavy wire leader (below).

Pike are strong fighters, usually making several powerful runs before coming to the net. They tend to fight deep but, on occasion, a hooked pike will make a spectacular jump.

Because of the pike's aggressive nature, catch-and-release is important. Otherwise, pike are quickly removed from the population before they reach a decent size. In heavily fished pike waters, anglers have trouble catching anything but small, 1- to 2-pound "hammerhandles."

Be sure to use a wire leader when fishing pike, muskies or pickerel. All members of the pike family have sharp-edged teeth that will easily shear off plain mono or even superline.

Use a "quick-strike" rig when fishing pike with large baitfish. This way, when you get a bite, you can set the hook right away rather than waiting for the fish to swallow the bait.

Pike are sight feeders, so it pays to use flashy baits such as spoons and bucktail spinners. The flash will catch their attention from a distance, drawing them to your lure.

Before attempting to remove a hook from a pike's toothy mouth, open it with a jaw spreader.

MUSKELLUNGE

(Esox masquinongy)

Varieties

The genetic makeup of muskies is quite variable. There are three distinct color phases: barred, spotted and clear (p. 56). But these varieties are not considered true subspecies. Because of widespread muskie stocking, any of these color phases may be found throughout the muskie's range.

• *Also called muskie, maskinonge, lunge.*

Muskies have dark spots or bars on light greenish to silvery sides. Or they may be unmarked. The tail has sharper lobes and smaller spots than that of a northern pike, or it may have no spots. Shown above is a spotted muskie.

Understanding Freshwater Gamefish

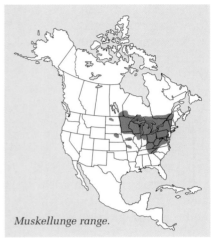

Muskellunge range.

newly-hatched muskies.

Muskies are classified as coolwater fish, preferring water in mid 60s to low 70s.

Feeding Habits

Fish makes up most of the diet, but muskies also eat frogs, mice, ducklings and even muskrats. They do not feed as aggressively as pike.

Although muskies and pike rarely hybridize in nature, hybrids, called tiger muskies, are commonly raised in hatcheries. Tiger muskies are more aggressive than pure-bred muskies, so they're easier to catch, but they don't grow quite as large.

Habitat

Muskies are found in weedy portions of natural lakes and in slow-moving, weedy rivers, but they seldom thrive in waters with an abundance of pike. The pike hatch earlier in the season and the young, larger pike prey upon the

Tiger muskies have light sides with dark, narrow, vertical bars, which are often broken into spots. The lobes of the tail are rounder than those of a true muskie.

Instead of grabbing whatever they see, they size up their prey carefully. They lie dormant until the moment is right and then attack quickly. Muskies are primarily daytime feeders, but they will also feed at night.

Spawning Behavior

Muskies spawn several weeks later than pike, at water temperatures in the upper 40s to upper 50s. They scatter their eggs in weedy bays, but may also spawn on weedy flats in the main lake. They do not make any attempt to guard the eggs or young.

Age/Growth

In warmwater lakes and streams, muskies may live up to 12 years. They have a much longer life span in colder waters, living as long as 30 years. A 20-pound

Typical Growth Rate

Age	Length (inches)	Weight (pounds)
1	11.0	—
2	17.6	1.5
3	24.1	3.1
4	28.5	5.1
5	32.8	9.0
6	35.5	12.5
7	38.6	14.8
9	42.8	21.2
11	46.1	25.0
13	49.0	29.9
15	51.4	33.4

muskie is likely to be about 10 years old.

World Record

69 pounds, 11 ounces; Chippewa Flowage, Wisconsin; October 20, 1949.

Other ID Features

Only the top half of a muskie's cheek and gill cover are scaled.

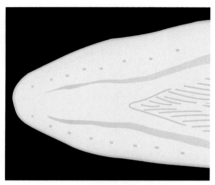

The underside of a muskie's lower jaw has 12 to 18 pores.

Other Muskie Varieties

Barred Muskie. *The light greenish to silvery sides have dark, wide vertical bars.*

Clear Muskie. *The sides are usually brownish or greenish with no vertical bars or spots.*

Fishing Facts

Experienced muskie anglers know that big baits catch big fish, so they commonly use lures measuring nearly a foot long. You'll need sturdy tackle to fish baits this size and to drive the hooks into the fishes' bony mouth.

Muskies are notorious followers, often chasing the bait up to the boat and then turning away at the last instant. But you can often make them strike by leaving a couple feet of line out, putting your rod tip in the water and making "figure eights" with your bait.

To preserve quality fishing, most muskie anglers practice catch-and-release. Always carry jaw spreaders and heavy longnose pliers. If possible, remove the hooks while the fish is still in the water.

When muskies are in dense weeds, try a spinnerbait. Retrieve it over a weedy flat, keeping it just above the weed tops. Or hold your rod tip high and reel fast enough that the blades slightly "bulge" the surface.

Large in-line spinners called "bucktails" are a favorite of many veteran muskie anglers. They are a good choice for fishing along weed edges or over weed tops, but they have open hooks so they do not work well in dense weeds.

Topwater lures, such as stickbaits and propbaits, are deadly for night fishing, especially in warm weather. The more noise and splash the lure produces, the better. Subsurface lures are a better choice when the water is cool.

CHAIN PICKEREL

(Esox niger)

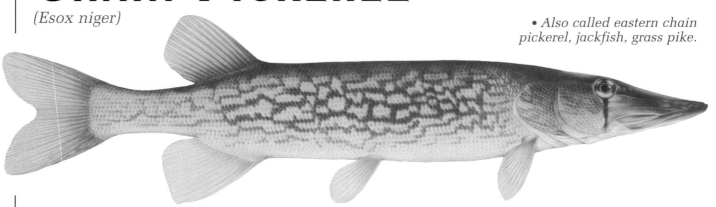

• *Also called eastern chain pickerel, jackfish, grass pike.*

Chain pickerel have a greenish to bronze background coloration with a dark chain-link pattern, explaining the name "chain pickerel." The entire cheek and gill cover are scaled and there are 8 pores on the underside of the lower jaw.

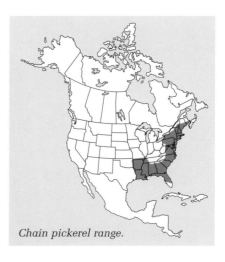

Chain pickerel range.

Varieties

Chain pickerel sometimes hybridize with redfin pickerel and northern pike.

Habitat

Found mainly in clear, weedy lakes, ponds and reservoirs, but also in slow-moving reaches of warmwater streams. Chain pickerel prefer water temperatures in the upper 70s.

Feeding Habits

The diet consists primarily of fish, but chain pickerel will eat whatever food they can find, as long as it is the right size. Some of the items found in their stomachs include frogs, crayfish,

Typical Growth Rate

Age	Length (inches)	Weight (pounds)
1	6.0	–
2	11.4	–
3	15.8	.9
4	19.1	1.4
5	21.7	2.2
6	23.6	3.3
7	24.8	4.4
8	25.7	5.4

mice and even snakes. Pickerel do most of their feeding in daylight hours.

Spawning Behavior

In early spring, chain pickerel move into shallow, weedy bays of lakes, connecting sloughs and river backwaters to spawn. When the water temperature reaches the mid 40's, they drape gelatinous strings of eggs up to 3 feet long over vegetation and bottom debris. The parents make no attempt to protect the eggs or fry.

Age/Growth

Chain pickerel may live up to 9 years, but they seldom reach a weight of more than 4 pounds. They generally grow faster in lakes than in streams.

World Record

9 pounds, 6 ounces; Guest Millpond, Georgia; February 17, 1961.

Fishing Facts

These aggressive biters will attack any kind of lure, particularly those that have plenty of action or flash, such as spinners and weedless spoons. They'll also hit crankbaits, jigs and topwaters, and fly fishermen catch them on big streamers. Whatever type of lure you select, be sure to attach a wire leader. Like pike and muskies, chain pickerel have razor-sharp teeth that will make short work of monofilament line or even superline.

When fishing in lily pads or other dense weedy cover, use a weedless spoon tipped with a strip of pork rind. The lure will snake through the weeds without hanging up, and pickerel find the action hard to resist.

Look for chain pickerel around floating-leaf vegetation, such as lily pads. Vegetation of this type not only provides shade and overhead protection, it also keeps the water slightly cooler.

CATFISH FAMILY

It's obvious where the catfish family (*Ictaluridae*) got its name. The fish have a prominent set of cat-like whiskers, or *barbels*, on their snout. Catfish use these barbels, which are equipped with numerous taste buds, to comb the bottom for food. Despite the fact that catfish have relatively poor eyesight, their barbels and strong sense of smell enable them to easily find food, even in muddy water or at night. Catfish can also be easily identified by their scaleless body and trout-like adipose fin on the rear of their back.

The catfish family has 39 members in the United States and Canada, but only 7 are commonly targeted by anglers. These include 4 species of catfish (channel, flathead, blue and white) and 3 species of bullheads (black, brown and yellow). The other members consist mainly of *madtoms*, which reach only a few inches in length.

All members of the catfish family are warmwater fish and are found in many of the same waters as members of the sunfish family. Bullheads are known for their tolerance of low oxygen levels but catfish are much less tolerant of such conditions.

Like sunfish, catfish are nest builders. Some species excavate a depression on the bottom, but others nest in holes in the bank. The male guards the nest and stays with the fry until they are ready to leave.

Understanding Freshwater Gamefish

CHANNEL CATFISH

(Ictalurus punctatus)

• *Also called blue channel cat, spotted cat, lady cat, fork-tail cat.*

Channel catfish range.

Channel cats are easy to recognize by their deeply-forked tail and their prominent upper jaw, which protrudes well past the lower, particularly on large males. The sides are bluish to greenish gray with a silvery tinge. Channel cats resemble blue cats, explaining why they're often called "blue channel cats," but the anal fin of a channel is shorter and more rounded than that of a blue.

Habitat

Channel catfish thrive in medium- to large-size rivers with slow to moderate current, but they are also found in shallow- to mid-depth reservoirs and in small lakes and ponds. Channels will not tolerate as much current as blue cats. They prefer a clean sand, gravel or rubble bottom with an abundance of cover such as log jams, wing dams or brush piles. They're commonly found in tailrace areas where there is an abundance of food.

The native range of the channel catfish extends from the Appalachian Mountains west to the Rockies, and from the Hudson Bay drainage south to the Gulf of Mexico. Their preferred temperature range, 75 to 80°F, is slightly lower than that of flatheads and blues. This explains why their native range extends farther north. Channel cats have been widely stocked in the United States, particularly in western reservoirs.

Feeding Habits

Of all the catfish species, channels have the least selective food habits. They will take live fish as well as dead or rotting fish, and will also eat larval aquatic insects, terrestrial insects, crayfish, crabs, snails, clams and even

Juvenile channel cats, called "fiddlers," have numerous black spots which usually disappear by the time the fish mature.

aquatic plants. Channel cats tend to consume more fish as they grow older; they reach the largest size in waters where fish make up the bulk of their diet.

Channel cats may feed at any time of the day or night, but veteran catfishermen know that feeding is heaviest after sundown. Channels are also known for their habit of gorging themselves when the water starts to rise. Feeding activity slows at water temperatures below 50°F.

Spawning Behavior

Channel cats spawn in late spring, usually at water temperatures between 70 and 75°F. Like other cats, they're difficult to find at spawning time. They build their nests in dark, secluded spots, such as holes in the bank, sunken barrels or alongside boulders or logs. Males protect the nest until the young disperse.

Age/Growth

Channel cats have been known to live more than 20 years, but the usual life span is 10 years or less. In the North, it takes 7 to 9 years for a channel cat to reach 3 pounds. In the South, they reach that size in only 4 or 5 years. Most channel cats taken by anglers range from 1 to 10 pounds, with 2- to 4-pounders being most common. As is true with most catfish, male and female channel cats grow to roughly the same size.

World Record

58 pounds; Santee-Cooper Reservoir, South Carolina; July 7, 1964.

Where to Find Channel Cats

Look for channel cats in deep holes along outside bends in big rivers and reservoirs.

Channel cats are commonly found in tailrace areas because of the abundance of food.

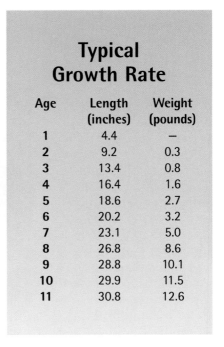

Typical Growth Rate

Age	Length (inches)	Weight (pounds)
1	4.4	–
2	9.2	0.3
3	13.4	0.8
4	16.4	1.6
5	18.6	2.7
6	20.2	3.2
7	23.1	5.0
8	26.8	8.6
9	28.8	10.1
10	29.9	11.5
11	30.8	12.6

Understanding Freshwater Gamefish

Fishing Facts

Willing biters, channel cats respond to "stinkbaits" better than flatheads or blues. They can also be attracted by chumming, usually with rotten cheese or fermented grain. Besides stinkbaits, channels can be taken on dried blood, chicken liver, worms, minnows and even artificial lures such as jigs and spinners. Once hooked, a channel cat wages a strong, determined battle in deep water.

Form paste baits, dough baits, cheese baits, blood baits and chicken liver around a treble hook with a wire coil to help hold them in place.

Wrap delicate baits such as chicken livers or entrails or putrefied fish in a mesh bag made from a nylon stocking or piece of cheesecloth. Push a single hook through the bag.

Ice fishermen on northern lakes and rivers sometimes catch channel cats on jigging lures, particularly jigging spoons and swimming minnows tipped with a minnow head.

Chum your fishing spot with a commercially-made chum block at least one day before you start fishing. Attach a rope to the block and lower it to the bottom. You can also tie it off to a bridge or tree limb. Some blocks last for 6 to 8 days.

FLATHEAD CATFISH

(Pylodictis olivaris)

• *Also called yellow cat, mud cat, shovelhead cat, appaluchion.*

As its name suggests, the flathead has a broad, flattened forehead. Its mottled, brownish-yellow coloration accounts for its common name, "yellow cat." The squarish tail and protruding lower jaw make the flathead easy to distinguish from other large North American catfish species, all of which have forked tails and underslung lower jaws. Its tiny eyes also give the flathead a distinctive look.

Habitat

Flatheads inhabit large river systems, including any impoundments and major tributaries. Although they are commonly called "mud cats," they seldom frequent areas with a soft bottom. River-dwelling flatheads spend most of their time in large, sluggish pools with a sandy or gravelly bottom or in the food-rich tailwaters of dams. In impoundments, you'll often find flatheads around flooded timber, stumps, or in tangles of woody cover.

Flatheads prefer water temperatures in the upper 70s to low 80s and can tolerate temperatures of more than 90°F. Contrary to popular belief, they are not able to survive in highly-polluted waters or in waters with extremely low dissolved oxygen levels.

Feeding Habits

An extremely efficient predator, the flathead has broad, powerful jaws with a large pad of tiny recurved teeth on the upper jaw that makes it virtually impossible for prey to escape once the fish clamps down on it.

Flatheads have a tooth pad on the roof of their mouth.

The flathead's diet consists mainly of live fish, but it also eats crayfish and clams. Unlike channel catfish, flatheads rarely consume rotten food. This explains why fishermen targeting flatheads use fresh, lively baitfish such as suckers, carp, large shiners and sunfish, or fresh cut bait rather than the "stink baits" and other prepared baits that work so well for channel cats.

Flatheads are secretive, solitary fish. They feed mainly at night, moving from secure cover in a deep pool to

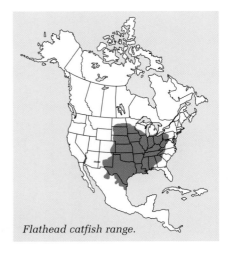

Flathead catfish range.

forage in shallow riffle areas. After feeding, an adult flathead returns to its favorite resting spot where it remains until the next night unless disturbed.

Spawning Behavior

Flatheads spawn in late spring or early summer, a little later than channel cats. Spawning usually takes place at water temperatures in the low to upper 70s. The fish often spawn in a natural hole in the bank, but they may excavate nests near logs or boulders.

Age/Growth

It's not unusual for flatheads to live 15 years, and

some individuals probably live much longer. Of all the North American catfish, only the blue cat reaches a larger size.

World Record

123 pounds; Elk City Reservoir, Kansas; May 14, 1998.

Typical Growth Rate

Age	Length (inches)	Weight (pounds)
1	7.5	—
3	18.2	2.6
5	23.2	6.0
7	29.5	12.8
9	33.4	19.1
11	37.5	26.2
13	40.5	33.0
15	43.0	42.1

Fishing Facts

One of the strongest fighting freshwater fish, the flathead typically wages a determined battle in deep water. You struggle to pull the fish up a few feet, then it retreats to the bottom and you start all over. It's not surprising that serious flathead anglers use pool-cue rods and 50-pound line. In much of the South, jug fishing, trotlining and noodling account for more flatheads than does rod-and-reel fishing.

Flatheads feed heavily at night, especially in warm weather. In most waters, the biggest flatheads are taken after dark.

A big lively baitfish, such as a sucker or chub, makes excellent bait for flatheads. Some flathead specialists bait up with fish weighing as much as 2 pounds.

BLUE CATFISH
(Ictalurus furcatus)

• *Also called silver cat, blue channel cat.*

As their name suggests, these fish are bluish to grayish in color, although some individuals are silvery. Blues, with their deeply forked tail, resemble channel cats and are sometimes called "blue channel cats." But unlike channels, their sides are not spotted (even on small fish), and their anal fin is considerably longer, with a straighter edge. Blues are somewhat stockier than channels and their head is smaller compared to the rest of their body. The profile, from the dorsal fin forward, is straight and steeply sloped, giving the body a distinctive, wedge-shaped appearance.

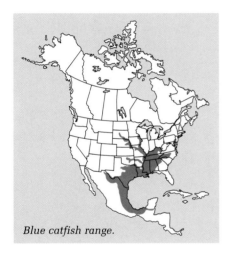

Blue catfish range.

Habitat

Blue cats are big-river fish, thriving in mainstem rivers and their major tributaries. They favor faster, clearer water than channel cats and are usually found over a clean sand, gravel or rubble bottom.

Blue catfish prefer water temperatures in the range of 77 to 82°F, slightly higher than the range of channel cats. Like channels, blues are often found in tailrace areas where food is abundant.

Blue catfish are native to the Mississippi, Missouri and Ohio river drainages in the central and southern states, and their range extends south into Mexico and northern Guatemala. Blues have been stocked in many reservoirs in both the eastern and western U.S., where they commonly grow to enormous sizes. In some impoundments, however, biologists believe that these fish fail to reproduce.

Blues can tolerate more salinity than channels or flatheads. In fact, tidewater rivers produce some of the largest blues.

America's blue catfish population has declined since 1900. Dam and lock construction along big rivers has blocked spawning runs, limiting the numbers of blues in many sections of the larger rivers. And by impounding the water, dams take away the current that blues prefer.

Feeding Habits

Blues tend to be more pelagic (open-water oriented) than other cats. They roam widely, often in great schools, foraging at any depth. Many commercial anglers report catching more blues on trotlines that are suspended under the surface than on those fished on the bottom.

Biologists consider blue cats "opportunistic" feeders, because they will eat whatever food is available. Although fish are the primary food of adult blues, they will also eat insects, crayfish and clams. Large blues do not hesitate to swallow fish weighing several pounds. In many southern reservoirs and rivers, the diet of blue catfish consists almost entirely of gizzard and threadfin shad.

Blue cats feed at any time of the day or night and, unlike other catfish species, they continue to feed heavily even when water temperatures dip into the 40°F range.

Spawning Behavior

Blues are more migratory than other catfish species. During the pre-spawn period, they often migrate upriver in large numbers, congregating in enormous schools below dams that block their spawning run. But as winter approaches, they commonly run downriver in search of warmer water.

Spawning takes place in late spring or early summer, usually at water temperatures from 70 to 75°F. Blues, like channels, nest in some type of cavity that provides shade and protection from predators. Common spawning sites includes undercut banks, root wads, depressions in the bottom and sheltered areas behind boulders.

Age/Growth

Blue cats are the largest North American catfish species. In the mid 1800s, when commercial catfishing was a booming industry along the Mississippi River, blues no doubt reached weights approaching 200 pounds.

Blues live longer than other catfish. The largest specimens are usually more than 20 years old. Growth varies greatly in different bodies of water, depending on forage availability. In the Louisiana Delta, for example, blues grow to 33.4 inches (about 17 pounds) in only 6 years. In Lake Chickamauga, Tennessee, they reach only 1.2 pounds in the same amount of time. Most blue catfish taken by today's anglers are in the 3- to 15-pound range.

Where to Find Blue Catfish

Blue cats are the most current-oriented catfish species. Look for them in areas of moderate to medium-fast current.

Blue cats often congregate on the upstream lip of a deep hole. There, they have the first chance at any food that drifts into the hole.

	Typical Growth Rate	
Age	Length (inches)	Weight (pounds)
1	5.9	—
2	10.0	0.4
3	13.9	0.9
4	17.4	1.6
5	21.1	3.3
6	25.9	7.4
7	30.2	12.4
8	34.4	19.8
9	40.3	33.9
10	42.0	40.5
11	44.1	47.4

World Record

111 pounds; Wheeler Reservoir, Alabama; July 5, 1996. Several other blues over 100 pounds have been caught and officially weighed in recent years.

Fishing Facts

Blue cats offer anglers something that few other freshwater gamefish can: the possibility of catching a 100-pound plus fish. In the 1800s, blues reached much larger sizes; one reportedly weighed in at 315 pounds.

Blues will take a variety of live baits, cut baits and prepared baits. In addition to hook-and-line fishing, blues are commonly taken by jug fishing and trotlining.

But commercial fishing has taken its toll on the largest blues. Some states, like Missouri, are now taking steps to eliminate commercial harvest so that more trophy blues are available to sport fishermen.

Blue cats are considered excellent eating; they have white, flaky, mild-tasting meat.

One of the most popular set-ups for blue cats is a slip-sinker rig baited with a piece of cut shad or herring. Use a 1-ounce egg sinker, a barrel swivel, a 12-inch leader and a size 3/0 to 5/0 wide-bend hook.

When fishing in current, use a slip-sinker rig with a flattened weight. If you attempt to use an ordinary egg sinker, it will roll in the current.

Stagger the depths of your lines when fishing for blues. The smaller, more numerous fish usually run shallowest; the biggest fish, deepest. It's not unusual to catch giant blues in water more than 50 feet deep.

WHITE CATFISH

(Ameiurus catus)

• *Also called Potomac cat, fork-tailed cat.*

White catfish bear a close resemblance to channel cats, but do not grow nearly as large. The tail is not quite as deeply forked, the body is never spotted, the anal fin is shorter (19 to 23 rays) and the chin barbels are white, rather than black or brown. Whites often possess the greenish- or bluish-silver coloration of the channel cat, but there is usually a sharper demarcation between the darker color of the sides and the whitish belly. Some whites are mottled with milky, pale gray to dark blue splotches.

Habitat

White catfish prefer slow current and are commonly found in sluggish streams, marshes, bayous, river backwaters, ponds and reservoirs.

Compared to other catfish species, they are more tolerant of a soft, silty bottom and high water temperatures. Their preferred temperature range is 80 to 85°F. White cats can also tolerate more salinity than other catfish species, so they are often found in the lower reaches of coastal rivers where other cats are absent.

The white catfish is sometimes called the "Potomac cat," because it was once limited to the Atlantic coastal states—from Chesapeake Bay to Florida—and a few of the gulf states. Whites have been successfully introduced into many waters in California and Nevada, as well as into numerous fee-fishing lakes across the country.

Feeding Habits

White catfish are gluttonous feeders. Although small fish are their favorite food item, they will also take fish eggs, aquatic insects, crustaceans and even pondweeds.

Although white catfish may feed at night, they are not as nocturnal as the other catfish species.

Spawning Behavior

Like other catfish, white cats spawn in late spring or early summer, generally at

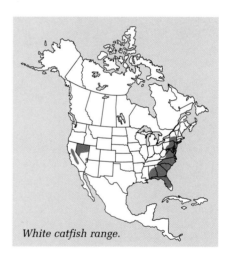

White catfish range.

water temperatures in the 70- to 75°F range. They build a large nest, usually on a sandbar, and the male guards the eggs and fry.

Age/Growth

White catfish may live up to 14 years, but their growth rate is the slowest of all the catfish species. In the northern part of their range, it takes from 9 to 11 years for a white cat to reach 2 pounds; in the South they normally reach that size in 6 or 7 years.

Fishing Facts

Even ardent catmen may not be familiar with these small catfish because their native range is so limited. And where white cats coexist with channel cats, anglers often fail to make the distinction. But white catfish are gaining in popularity as stocking expands their range. Whites are scrappy fighters, but their relatively small size limits their popularity in regions where anglers have access to bigger cats. An excellent table fish, the white catfish has firm, white flesh.

Because of their willingness to bite during daylight hours and to take most any kind of bait, white cats have become very popular in fee-fishing lakes and ponds.

The majority of white cats caught by anglers weigh from 1 to 3 pounds.

World Record

22 pounds; William Land Park Pond, California; March 21, 1994.

Typical Growth Rate

Age	Length (inches)	Weight (pounds)
1	4.8	—
2	6.3	—
3	8.4	0.2
4	10.3	0.4
5	12.3	0.7
6	13.4	0.9
7	14.8	1.3
8	16.1	1.8
9	18.0	2.3
10	21.1	3.7

BLACK BULLHEAD

(Ameiurus melas)

• Also called yellowbelly bullhead, horned pout.

Black bullheads have dark greenish to goldish sides and dark-colored barbels. They are sometimes confused with brown bullheads, but the tail is slightly notched, there is a pale, crescent-shaped bar at the base of the tail and their pectoral spines (behind each gill) are not as strongly barbed (p. 75).

Habitat

Black bullheads are most abundant in lakes and streams with turbid water, a muddy bottom and very little current. They favor water temperatures in the 75 to 85°F range.

Often the dominant species in freeze-out lakes, black bullheads can tolerate dissolved-oxygen levels lower than can any other freshwater gamefish, with the possible exception of the yellow bullhead.

Feeding Habits

The diet consists of a wide variety of foods including small fish, fish eggs, worms, leeches, molluscs, insects and plant material.

Spawning Behavior

Black bullheads spawn in late spring or early summer at water temperatures in the upper 60s. The female builds a nest in weedy or woody cover and, after spawning, she helps the male guard the eggs and young. After the young leave the nest, they can often be seen swimming along the shoreline in tight schools.

Age/Growth

Black bullheads are the most common bullhead species and are often so abundant that they become stunted. Although they live up to 10 years, their growth rate is highly variable.

If stunting is not a problem, black bullheads grow to respectable size. In fact, the world record for the black bullhead (8 pounds, 15 ounces) is larger than that of any other bullhead species.

A black bullhead in the North usually reaches a weight of 1 pound in 7 to 9

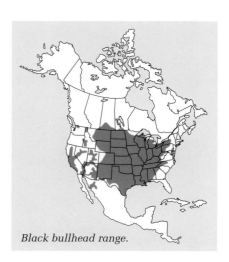

Black bullhead range.

Typical Growth Rate

Age	Length (inches)	Weight (pounds)
1	4.5	—
2	6.6	—
3	8.6	0.3
4	9.9	0.6
5	10.5	0.8
6	12.6	1.2
7	14.3	1.7
8	15.8	2.2

years; in the South, only 4 or 5 years.

World Record

8 pounds, 15 ounces; Sturgis Pond, Michigan; July 19, 1987.

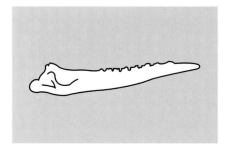

Black bullheads have pectoral spines with tiny barbs that don't catch on your thumb and finger when you run them along it.

Fishing Facts

Black bullheads are not fussy; you can catch them on most any bait including worms, cheesebait, stinkbait liver and even chunks of soap.

Even though black bullheads are weak fighters, their tasty white meat makes them popular with many anglers.

Because they are able to tolerate such low oxygen levels, black bullheads can survive in shallow, fertile, weed-choked lakes that are prone to winterkill.

Grip a bullhead as shown to remove the hook, being careful to avoid getting poked by the pectoral or dorsal spines, which have a weak venom and can inflict a painful wound.

BROWN BULLHEAD

(Ameiurus nebulosus)

• *Also called red cat, creek cat and horned pout.*

Northern brown bullheads have yellowish to brownish sides with light mottling. The tail is square or has only a very slight notch. The pectoral spines are more sharply barbed than those of a black bullhead and there is no pale crescent-shaped mark at the base of the tail.

Varieties

There are two recognized subspecies: the southern brown bullhead (*Ameiurus nebulosus marmoratus*) and the northern brown bullhead (*Ameiurus nebulosus nebulosus*).

Habitat

Brown bullheads are usually found in larger, deeper lakes than other bullhead species. They also thrive in some smaller lakes and ponds, and in slow-moving streams, but they are not as resistant to low oxygen levels as black bullheads. Browns favor water temperatures in the upper 70s or low 80s.

Feeding Habits

The diet of the brown bull-head is similar to that of the black, consisting of small fish, fish eggs, worms, leeches, molluscs, crayfish, insects and plant material.

Spawning Behavior

Spawning takes place in late spring or early summer, generally at water temperatures in the low 70s. Both parents build a nest on a mud or sand bottom, usually among roots, logs or other cover that provides shade. After spawning, they continue to guard the nest and protect the young.

Age/Growth

Brown bullheads may live up to 12 years, but the usual life span is much shorter. In the northern part of the range,

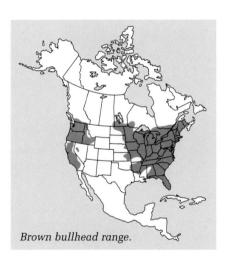

Brown bullhead range.

Typical Growth Rate

Age	Length (inches)	Weight (pounds)
1	4.3	—
2	7.2	0.2
3	9.9	0.5
4	11.3	0.8
5	12.6	1.0
6	14.2	1.5
7	16.0	2.1

The southern brown bullhead has more distinct mottling than the northern brown bullhead.

it takes 7 or 8 years to grow a 1-pounder; in the southern part, only 4 or 5.

World Record

6 pounds, 2 ounces; Pearl River, Mississippi; January 19, 1991.

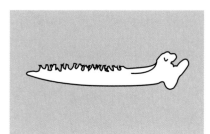

Brown bullheads have a strongly-barbed pectoral spine that catches your thumb and forefinger when you run them along it.

Fishing Facts

Brown bullheads are easy to catch. Most anglers use worms, but minnows, pieces of shrimp and stinkbaits also work well. Although browns are not strong fighters, they'll give you a little more tussle than a black. Their meat is reddish or pinkish, rather than white, but it is quite firm and has a good flavor.

Brown bullheads are most common in medium-depth warmwater lakes with moderate fertility and weed growth.

Smear paste-type stinkbait bait onto a soft-plastic "ringworm." The ridges in the plastic help hold the bait in place.

YELLOW BULLHEAD

(Ameiurus natalis)

• *Also called white-whiskered bullhead, yellow cat.*

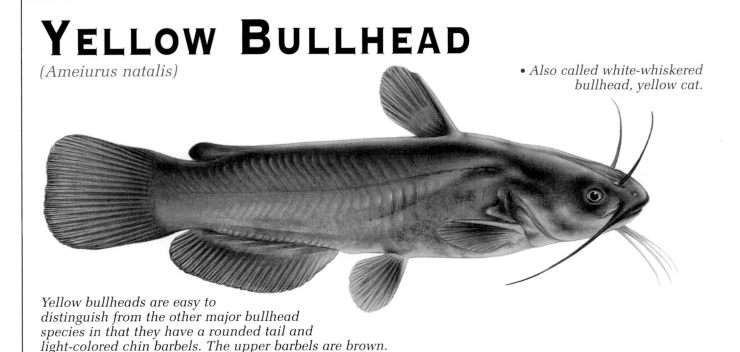

Yellow bullheads are easy to distinguish from the other major bullhead species in that they have a rounded tail and light-colored chin barbels. The upper barbels are brown.

Habitat

Although bullheads are usually considered a muddy-water fish, yellow bullheads prefer clear water with a heavy growth of aquatic vegetation. But they can tolerate polluted water and extremely low dissolved oxygen levels.

Yellow bullheads thrive in warm, slow-moving streams; ponds; small, weedy lakes; and weedy bays of larger lakes. Their preferred temperature range is 75 to 80°F.

Feeding Habits

The yellow bullhead's diet is not much different from that of other bullheads, but yellows are known for their habit of scavenging most any kind of organic matter off the bottom. They will eat bits of weeds, aquatic insects and other invertebrates and, on occasion, live fish.

Spawning Behavior

Spawning takes place in late spring or early summer,

when the water temperature warms to the upper 60s or low 70s. The fish may nest in a cavity in the bank or dig out a depression in a clean bottom. When spawning has been completed, the male guards the nest until the eggs hatch and the fry disperse. Yellows have a lower reproductive rate than blacks, meaning that they're less prone to stunting.

Age/Growth

Yellow bullheads grow more rapidly than blacks or browns, but their life span seldom exceeds 7 years. There is little difference in growth rate from north to south. It takes about 5 years to grow a 1 pounder in the northern part of the range and about 4 years in the southern part.

World Record

4 pounds, 8 ounces; Mormon Lake, Arizona; July 15, 1989.

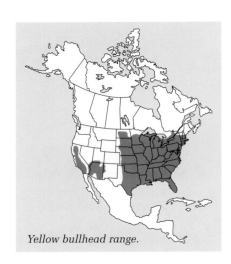

Yellow bullhead range.

Typical Growth Rate

Age	Length (inches)	Weight (pounds)
1	2.5	—
2	6.2	0.2
3	10.3	0.5
4	11.9	0.9
5	14.0	1.4
6	15.9	2.0

Fishing Facts

Look for yellow bullheads in warmwater streams with relatively clear water and some weed growth.

Carry a hemostat in case a bullhead swallows your bait. Because their jaws are so strong, it's nearly impossible to remove a hook with your fingers.

TEMPERATE BASS FAMILY

The term "temperate bass" is somewhat of a misnomer because it implies that these fish prefer intermediate water temperatures. In fact, all members of the temperate bass family (*Moronidae*) are warmwater fish, favoring water temperatures above the 70°F mark. Temperate bass are also called "true bass," a term that distinguishes them from the black bass (p. 5).

Temperate bass differ from black bass in that they are random spawners rather than nest builders. They deposit their eggs in moving water and then let them drift with the current. Most members of the family have a silvery coloration and all but the white perch have dark horizontal stripes along the sides.

The temperate bass family has only 4 members that inhabit fresh waters of the United States and Canada. Two (white bass and yellow bass) are solely freshwater species and two (striped bass and white perch) are anadromous, spending most of their life at sea or in coastal estuaries and spawning in coastal streams. White perch are also found in inland lakes and striped bass have been stocked in fresh water in more than 2 dozen states.

Most temperate bass are pack feeders. They surround a school of baitfish and herd it to the surface, feeding frantically for a few minutes and then moving on when the baitfish school breaks up.

WHITE BASS

(Morone chrysops)

• *Also called striper, sand bass, silver bass.*

White bass have silvery sides with black horizontal stripes that are unbroken above the lateral line but broken in an irregular pattern below. The body is deeper than that of a striped bass and there is a single patch of teeth on the tongue, rather than two patches. The dorsal fins differ from those of a yellow bass in that they are not joined at the base, and the lower jaw is considerably longer than the upper.

Varieties

White bass sometimes hybridize naturally with yellow bass. Striped-white bass hybrids called wipers (p. 85) are produced in hatcheries and stocked throughout the southern U.S.

Habitat

Big-river systems, including connecting lakes, make ideal habitat for white bass. They are most numerous in large bodies of water with an abundance of open-water forage such as shad. White bass prefer water temperatures from the mid 60s to mid 70s.

Feeding Habits

White bass commonly feed in packs, herding schools of open-water baitfish, such as shad and emerald shiners, to the surface. White bass also eat crustaceans, immature aquatic insects and a variety of other small baitfish. Feeding takes place at any time of the day or night, but is heaviest around dusk and dawn.

Spawning Behavior

In spring, when the water temperature reaches the upper 50s or low 60s, huge schools of white bass swim upriver to spawn below a dam or other migration barrier. The eggs are deposited on sand-gravel shoals with light current and then abandoned. White bass occasionally spawn in shoal areas of lakes or at the mouths of tributary streams.

Age/Growth

White bass normally grow to about 1½ pounds in 5 years. They seldom live longer than than 6 years.

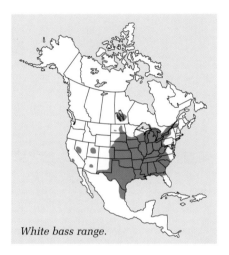

White bass range.

Typical Growth Rate

Age	Length (inches)	Weight (pounds)
1	5.5	—
2	9.8	0.4
3	12.0	0.8
4	13.1	1.1
5	14.1	1.5
6	14.9	1.7

World Record

6 pounds, 7 ounces; Saginaw Bay, Michigan; September 19, 1989.

Fishing Facts

White bass are easiest to catch in spring, when they congregate below dams to spawn, and in late summer and fall, when they begin their pack-feeding behavior. Keep your boat away from a feeding pack or you'll spook them. You can catch white bass on any lure about the size of a shad, but the best choice is one with a single hook; that way, you can unhook the fish quickly and get your lure back into the water.

Look for circling gulls to help pinpoint packs of white bass feeding on shad. When the fish start feeding, you'll see the gulls diving to grab the injured baitfish.

Tie a pair of jigs onto a 3-way swivel rig, using 10-pound-test leaders. This way, you can catch two white bass at a time without breaking one of the leaders.

STRIPED BASS

(Morone saxatilis)

• *Also called striper, rockfish.*

Striped bass have silvery sides with 7 or 8 horizontal stripes that are unbroken. The body is more elongated than that of a white bass and there are two patches of teeth on the tongue, rather than a single patch.

Striped bass range.

Varieties

Hybrids can be produced by crossing male white bass and female striped bass. Called wipers, these popular fish are stocked in many southern waters.

Habitat

Striped bass are an anadromous species, spending most of their life at sea and entering freshwater streams to spawn. But stripers are also capable of living solely in fresh water and have been widely stocked, mainly in southern reservoirs.

Striped bass prefer water temperatures from the mid 60s to the mid 70s and are considered warmwater gamefish. They thrive in large reservoirs with an ample supply of open-water forage, particularly shad.

Feeding Habits

Like white bass, stripers are known for their pack-feeding behavior. Although fish make up most of the diet, they also eat crustaceans and a variety of aquatic insects.

Stripers may feed all day long, especially in cloudy weather, but they're most aggressive early and late in the day. Feeding activity drops off greatly at water temperatures below 50°F.

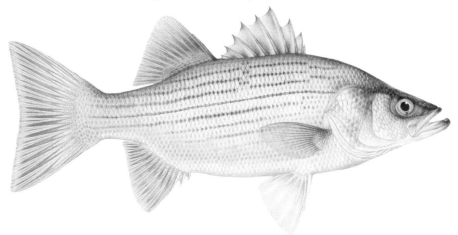

Wipers have stripes that are broken above and below the lateral line. The body is deeper than that of a striper but not as deep as that of a white bass. **World Record:** *27 pounds, 5 ounces; Greer's Ferry Lake, Arkansas; April 24, 1997.*

Spawning Behavior

Striped bass spawn in spring, generally at water temperatures in the upper 50s. Reservoir stripers usually ascend the main river channel to spawn in the tailwaters of the upstream dam. It's not uncommon to see dozens of fish rolling together in shallow water as they deposit their eggs. They generally choose a spawning site with light to moderate current and scatter their eggs at random. The moving water is necessary to keep the semi-buoyant eggs afloat; otherwise they would settle to the bottom and suffocate. Stripers do not guard their eggs or fry.

Where to Find Striped Bass

Tailwaters of dams draw spawning stripers from downstream reservoirs. Look for the fish in slow current along the edges of the fast water.

Look for stripers along edges of timbered flats. The trees serve as a "wall" against which the fish can push schools of shad.

Age/Growth

Striped bass grow faster, live longer and reach a much larger size than white bass. A striper may attain a weight of 10 pounds in only five years, and they sometimes live 20 years or more.

Striped bass grow to a larger size in salt water than in fresh water. Commercial fishermen off the Atlantic coast once netted a striper that weighed 125 pounds.

World Records

Landlocked striped bass: 67 pounds, 8 ounces; O'Neill Forebay, California; May 7, 1992.

Saltwater striped bass: 78 pounds, 8 ounces; Atlantic City, New Jersey; September 21, 1982.

Typical Growth Rate

Age	Length (inches)	Weight (pounds)
1	9.1	0.3
2	16.5	2.1
3	21.0	4.3
4	24.7	7.0
5	28.0	10.2
6	30.5	12.9
7	32.8	15.2
8	34.9	18.1
9	36.3	20.7
10	37.8	24.9

Fishing Facts

Striped bass and wipers rank among the strongest-fighting freshwater gamefish. Because they're often found near heavy cover, you'll need sturdy tackle. Most anglers use 20- to 30-pound-class baitcasting gear.

You can jump-fish for striped bass and wipers just as you would for white bass, but you'll need considerably larger lures, including minnowbaits, poppers and horsehead jigs tipped with curlytails.

Live shad also account for plenty of striped bass and wipers. You can slow-troll them or suspend them from a balloon to keep them swimming just above the tops of flooded timber, a favorite striper hangout.

Hook a live shad through the nostrils and use an electric trolling motor to move it along very slowly. Watch your depth finder for signs of fish or baitfish schools, and set your line to fish just above them.

Fish a shad beneath a balloon, keeping it just above the treetops. A balloon works much better than an ordinary float; because it has practically no water resistance, the shad can easily tow it around and cover more water.

Retrieve a large floating minnowbait just beneath the surface so it leaves a noticeable wake. This presentation is usually more effective than working the bait deeper.

When you've located some stripers but can't get them to bite, try a big popper. Jerk the lure sharply to make it throw water a foot into the air.

YELLOW BASS

(Morone mississippiensis)

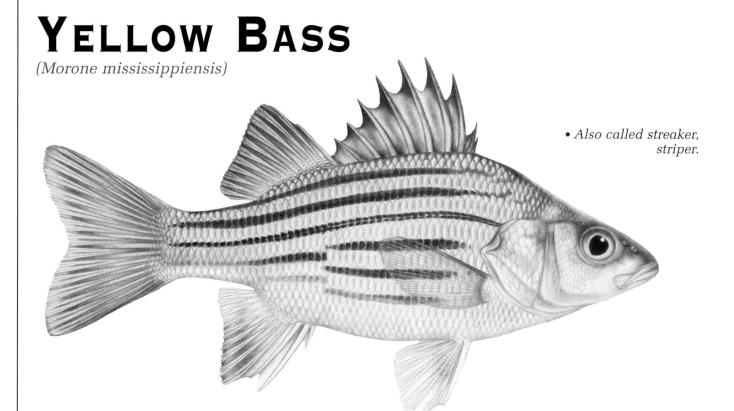

• *Also called streaker, striper.*

Yellow bass have yellowish to goldish sides with 6 or 7 black horizontal stripes that are very distinct. Yellow bass resemble white bass, but the stripes below the lateral line are broken just ahead of the anal fin, the dorsal fins are joined at the base and the lower jaw protrudes only slightly beyond the upper.

Varieties

Yellow bass sometimes hybridize with white bass.

Habitat

Yellow bass are primarily a southern species, although they can be found as far north as southern Minnesota and Wisconsin. They inhabit large rivers, including impoundments and backwater areas, but are also found in some natural lakes. They prefer large, weed-free expanses of open water and water temperatures in the upper 70s.

Feeding Habits

The diet includes zoo-plankton, immature aquatic insects and small fish such as gizzard shad and young-of-the-year of their own kind. Yellow bass usually feed on the bottom or in midwater—they rarely pack-feed on the surface. Sporadic feeding occurs throughout the day, but the fish feed most heavily around dawn and dusk.

Spawning Behavior

In spring, yellow bass swim upriver or into tributary streams to spawn. When the water temperature reaches the upper 50s or low 60s, they scatter their eggs on gravelly shoals, often the same ones used by white

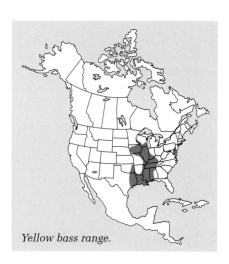

Yellow bass range.

bass. Yellow bass may also spawn in shallow shoal areas of lakes. They do not protect the eggs or fry.

Age/Growth

Yellow bass have a maximum life span of 7 years, but few live beyond 4. At that age, they usually weigh ½ to ¾ pound.

Typical Growth Rate

Age	Length (inches)	Weight (pounds)
1	3.9	—
2	7.8	0.4
3	8.8	0.5
4	9.7	0.6
5	10.8	0.8

World Record

2 pounds, 4 ounces; Lake Monroe, Louisiana; March 27, 1977.

Fishing Facts

Yellow bass are scrappy fighters for their size, and their firm, white meat is considered better eating than that of a white bass. Although they seldom pack-feed on the surface, they may feed that way in the mid-depths; once you locate a school, you can catch a lot of fish in a hurry using the small lures shown below.

Once you find the fish, stop the boat and cast to them using jigs, spinners, spoons or small crankbaits.

Locate schools of yellow bass by trolling with multiple lines set at various depths.

WHITE PERCH

(Morone americana)

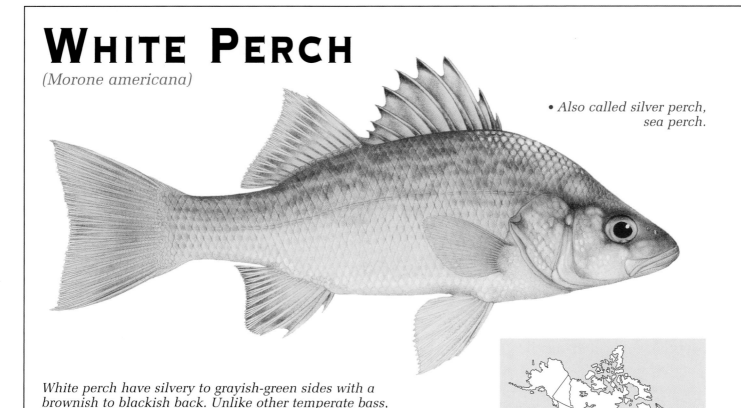

• *Also called silver perch, sea perch.*

White perch have silvery to grayish-green sides with a brownish to blackish back. Unlike other temperate bass, they do not have horizontal stripes.

Varieties

White perch occasionally hybridize with striped bass.

Habitat

Because they can tolerate fresh, salt or brackish water, white perch are found in a variety of habitats including warm, shallow lakes and reservoirs, tidal rivers and estuaries. They have also become established in warmwater portions of the Great Lakes. White perch prefer water temperatures in the upper 70s.

Feeding Habits

The diet consists mainly of immature aquatic insects, crustaceans and small fish. On occasion, white perch feed in packs, surrounding schools of baitfish and herding them to the surface, but they are less prone to pack-feeding than are white bass. White perch feed sporadically throughout the day, but the heaviest feeding takes place around sunset or after dark.

Spawning Behavior

In spring, anadromous white perch enter rivers along the Atlantic coast to spawn. Lake-dwelling populations usually spawn in tributary streams. When the water temperature is in the 50s, they randomly scatter their eggs over a variety of bottom types, usually in water less than 10 feet deep. The parents do not protect the eggs or fry.

Age/Growth

Although white perch may live up to 15 years, the normal life span is 5 to 7. In that time, they normally reach a weight of ½ to 1 pound.

White perch range.

Typical Growth Rate

Age	Length (inches)	Weight (pounds)
1	3.5	—
2	7.5	0.2
3	8.9	0.4
4	9.8	0.5
5	10.5	0.6
6	11.3	0.8
7	12.1	1.0

World Record

4 pounds, 12 ounces; Messalonskee Lake, Maine; June 4, 1949.

Fishing Facts

Although white perch run small in many waters, they are feisty fighters and excellent table fare. Willing biters, they readily take worms and minnows, as well as a variety of small artificials including spinners, spoons, jigs and small minnowbaits. Fly fishermen have good success on wet flies and small streamers.

After dark, set up a lantern on a pole or use a "crappie light" to attract white perch. The light draws plankton and insects which, in turn, draw minnows and, eventually, perch.

Tip a spinner with a small piece of worm when casting for white perch. When the fish are finicky, the bait sometimes makes a big difference.

STURGEON & PADDLEFISH FAMILY

Sturgeon and paddlefish are the most primitive gamefish in North America. Taxonomists believe that some of the sturgeon species that now exist date back nearly 100 million years.

The sturgeon family (*Acipenseridae*) and the paddlefish family (*Polyodontidae*) differ from other families of freshwater gamefish in that they have a cartilaginous, rather than bony, skeleton. Their body is scaleless and the spine extends through the long upper lobe of the tail, explaining their shark-like appearance.

Sturgeon are easy to recognize because of the rows of bony plates, or *scutes*, along the sides and the 4 long barbels beneath the snout. There are 7 species of sturgeon in the United States and Canada, 4 of which are anadromous, including the legendary white sturgeon.

These behemoths, which have been trapped by dams in some western rivers, have been known to reach weights exceeding 1000 pounds. The only species with an extensive inland range are the lake sturgeon and the much smaller shovelnose sturgeon.

As their name suggests, paddlefish have a huge paddle-like bill about 1/3 the length of their body. The skin is smooth, with no bony scutes. The paddlefish family has only 2 members, one of which is found in China.

LAKE STURGEON

(Acipenser fulvescens)

• *Also called rock sturgeon.*

Lake sturgeon have brownish to grayish sides with bony plates or "scutes" along the lateral line. Lake sturgeon lack the white spots of the white sturgeon (p. 96) and the barbels are located farther from the tip of the snout.

Habitat

Lake sturgeon inhabit large rivers and lakes connected to them. Primarily bottom dwellers, they are usually found at depths of 30 feet or less, but have been taken in water more than 100 feet deep. Lake sturgeon prefer water temperatures in the low to mid 60s.

Feeding Habits

Lake sturgeon swim along with their barbels combing the bottom. When the barbels feel a small food item, such as a snail, clam, crayfish or larval insect, the tubular mouth quickly juts out and sucks the morsel in along with silt, sand, gravel or other bottom materials, which are then expelled through the gills.

Spawning Behavior

Soon after ice-out, lake sturgeon begin their spawning migration. When the huge fish begin to congregate in pools near their spawning grounds, they can sometimes be seen leaping completely out of the water and landing with a noisy splash. When the water temperature reaches the low 50s, they scatter their eggs in swift water, often just below an impassible barrier. The parents do not protect the eggs or fry. An individual female spawns only once every 4 to 6 years.

Age/Growth

Lake sturgeon are extremely long-lived. Females do not become sexually mature until their early to mid-20s and may live up to 80 years. Males mature at 15 to 20 years of age and may live 50 years. There have been several reports of lake sturgeon exceeding 200 pounds.

World Record

168 pounds; Nottawasaga River, Ontario; May 29, 1982.

Lake sturgeon range.

Typical Growth Rate

Age	Length (inches)	Weight (pounds)
5	26.1	4.5
10	35.7	9.2
15	44.5	18.5
20	49.8	28.2
25	53.9	40.0
30	60.6	53.2
40	67.0	70.9
50	72.4	107.0

Fishing Facts

Powerful fighters and spectacular leapers, lake sturgeon require beefy tackle. Serious anglers use light salt-water gear spooled with 30- to 50-pound mono or superline. Most fish are taken on nightcrawlers or cut bait. Whether eaten fresh or smoked, the table quality is excellent, and the eggs make superb caviar.

Look for lake sturgeon in tailwaters of big-river dams. These food-rich areas hold fish from early spring through fall.

Bait up with a gob of nightcrawlers on a single hook. You may need as much as 6 ounces of weight to hold the bait in place in swift water.

WHITE STURGEON
(Acipenser transmontanus)

• *Also called Pacific sturgeon and Columbia sturgeon.*

White sturgeon have grayish to brownish sides, usually with white speckles. Like lake sturgeon, they have a row of bony plates (scutes) along the lateral line, but the barbels are closer to the tip of the snout.

Habitat

The majority of white sturgeon are anadromous. They live in estuaries of large rivers from California to Alaska, and ascend the rivers only to spawn. Some fish, however, have become established in the upper reaches of these rivers—sometimes more than 1,000 miles from the sea—and spend their entire life in fresh water. White sturgeon prefer water temperatures from 65 to 70°F.

Feeding Habits

Like most other sturgeon, whites comb the bottom with their barbels to find food. They eat small items like insect larvae, but fish are their primary food, followed by crayfish.

Spawning Behavior

White sturgeon usually enter their spawning streams in early spring. When the water temperature is in the low to upper 50s, they scatter their eggs in swift current, often below a rapids or impassible barrier. The parents do not guard the eggs or fry. An individual female spawns only once every 4 to 11 years.

Age/Growth

White sturgeon have a maximum life span of more than 100 years. They grow rapidly up to about age 35, but their growth rate then slows considerably. Weight gain continues, but there is only a minimal increase in length.

World Record

468 pounds; Carquinez Straights, California; July 9, 1983. Several larger ones have been caught and released and one historical

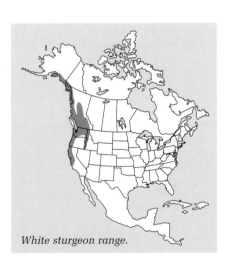

White sturgeon range.

account tells of a 1500-pounder taken on a trotline in the Snake River, Idaho, in 1898.

Typical Growth Rate

Age	Length (inches)	Weight (pounds)
5	30.5	8.6
10	42.2	16.1
15	52.4	26.8
20	63.2	56.3
25	76.8	106.9
30	92.1	183.0

Fishing Facts

White sturgeon are the largest fish that swim in North America's inland waters. To land one, you'll need heavy saltwater gear and 100-pound-test line. Popular baits include whole or cut fish, shrimp and gobs of nightcrawlers. In many white sturgeon waters, catch-and-release is mandatory.

Look for white sturgeon in deep pools below major rapids. Such areas hold a variety of the smaller fish that sturgeon eat.

Make a slip-sinker rig using a 10-ounce bell sinker and a tandem-hook harness tied with size 12/0 hooks. Rig a whole fish on the harness as shown; cast or drop it into the middle of the pool.

PADDLEFISH
(Polyodon spathula)

• *Also called spoonbill cat,
shovelnose cat.*

*Paddlefish have a long, flattened
paddle-like snout and a long, pointed gill
cover that extends almost to the middle of the body.
The sides and back vary from grayish to bluish-black.*

Habitat

Paddlefish inhabit large river systems, particularly wide lake-like reaches, backwaters and other slow-moving areas. They also congregate in the tailwaters of dams. Preferred water temperatures range from the mid 50s to low 60s.

Feeding Habits

Paddlefish are "filter" feeders, swimming about with their mouth agape and taking in water along with any plankton and insect life it contains. The food is removed by the fine gill rakers, and the water is expelled through the gills. Some people believe that paddlefish use their long bill to dislodge food from the bottom but, in reality, they use it to feel for tiny food items. When water temperatures reach the upper 60s in summer, paddlefish feed very little.

Spawning Behavior

In spring, when the river is rising and the water temperature is in the upper 40s or low 50s, paddlefish begin to spawn. The eggs are scattered onto shallow gravel bars, often in strong current, and then abandoned.

Age/Growth

Paddlefish are long-lived. Individuals up to 30 years of age have been documented. Young paddlefish grow very rapidly, often reaching a weight of 30 pounds or more in only 7 years. Older fish grow much more slowly.

World Record

142 pounds, 8 ounces; Missouri River, Montana; 1973.

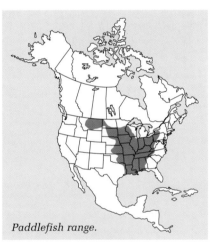

Paddlefish range.

Typical Growth Rate

Age	Length (inches)	Weight (pounds)
1	8.5	—
3	27.9	2.2
5	36.6	7.5
7	48.8	17.6
9	54.1	24.6
11	58.1	29.4
13	61.5	35.2
15	63.3	39.5

Fishing Facts

Paddlefish rarely strike baits or lures. In some waters, however, they can be legally snagged. These powerful fighters demand very heavy tackle and at least 80-pound-test line. Paddlefish have firm, white, tasty meat. It can be eaten fresh, but is usually smoked. The eggs are often used for caviar.

During the spring spawning period, anglers using heavy saltwater gear snag paddlefish below dams on large rivers. The fish must be tightly concentrated in order to have a reasonable chance of snagging one.

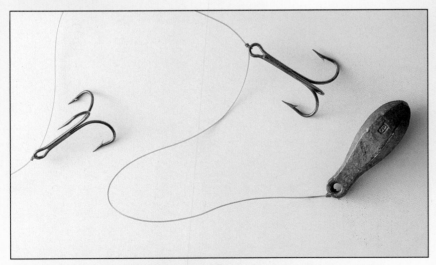

Make a snagging rig by tying on several large treble hooks spaced 1 to 3 feet apart and then attaching a heavy sinker to the end of the line.

HERRING FAMILY

Many freshwater fishermen are familiar with some of the smaller members of the herring family—such as gizzard shad, threadfin shad and skipjack herring—because they make excellent bait for catfish, striped bass and other large predator fish. The only members of the family targeted by freshwater anglers are the anadromous species: American shad, hickory shad and occasionally blueback herring.

The herring family (*Clupeidae*) consists of 40 species that inhabit United States and Canadian waters. Most of them are small fish (herring, sardines, menhaden, pilchards and anchovies) that spend their entire life at sea. One species, the alewife, entered the Great Lakes via the St. Lawrence Seaway and has become firmly established in those waters.

All members of the herring family have thin, silvery bodies. They resemble whitefish, but have a sharp keel on the belly and no adipose fin. They feed mainly on plankton, roaming open water in large schools, filtering the tiny morsels from the water with their gill rakers.

The American shad is by far the most popular member of the family, but its numbers have declined dramatically in many major rivers along the Atlantic coast. Thanks to stocking programs and fishing restrictions, however, shad are making a dramatic comeback in some of these waters.

AMERICAN SHAD

(Alosa sapidissima)

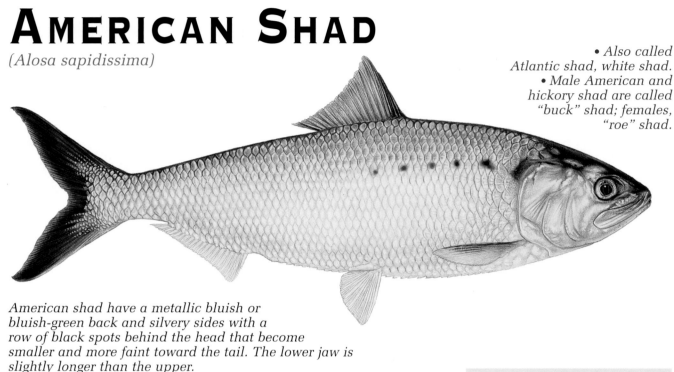

• Also called
Atlantic shad, white shad.
• Male American and
hickory shad are called
"buck" shad; females,
"roe" shad.

*American shad have a metallic bluish or
bluish-green back and silvery sides with a
row of black spots behind the head that become
smaller and more faint toward the tail. The lower jaw is
slightly longer than the upper.*

Close Relatives

Hickory shad (*Alosa
mediocris*) are considerably
smaller and much less common than American shad.

Habitat

American shad spend most
of their life at sea, entering
rivers and streams along the
Atlantic and Pacific coasts
during the spawning period.

Feeding Habits

The diet consists mainly of
zooplankton and insect larvae, although they occasionally eat small fish. Shad do
not feed while in fresh water,
although they do not hesitate
to strike lures—some say out
of annoyance.

Spawning Behavior

The timing of the spawning
run varies greatly, depending
on latitude. In Florida
streams, the run begins in

mid-November; in Canadian
streams, July. When the water
temperature reaches the low
60s, females release their eggs
into the current where they
are fertilized by several
males. Most spawning activity takes place after dark.

Age/Growth

American shad spawn for
the first time at age 2 to 5,

American shad range.

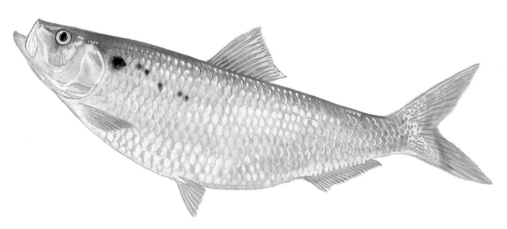

*Hickory shad resemble American shad, but the first black spot behind
the head is more distinct and the lower jaw is considerably longer
than the upper. Hickory shad seldom exceed 2 pounds.*

when they weigh 3 to 5 pounds. In the southern part of the range, shad usually die after spawning, but the number that survive increases farther northward. In northern streams, an individual shad may spawn up to 6 times. Repeat spawners usually weigh 5 to 9 pounds.

World Record

11 pounds, 4 ounces; Connecticut River, Massachusetts; May 19, 1986.

Typical Growth Rate

Age	Length (inches)	Weight (pounds)
1	7.9	—
2	12.5	.8
3	15.2	1.5
4	18.1	2.5
5	19.8	3.3
6	20.6	3.9
7	22.0	4.7
8	23.4	5.8

Fishing Facts

Fishing for American shad is usually best midway between high and low tide, when the current is strongest. Most anglers use spinning gear and a shad "dart," but the fish will also take subsurface flies. When you hook a shad, you're in for a spectacular fight. They usually make several cartwheels before coming to the net. Hickory shad, though smaller, are even better jumpers than American shad.

A shad dart is a small leadhead jig that has a flattened face to give it an erratic action. Using medium spinning gear, cast the jig along the edge of fast water and bump it along the bottom.

Look for American shad in fast water, especially where it flows around a point or over a gravel bar. Slack water seldom produces many fish.

TROUT FAMILY

The trout family (*Salmonidae*) includes North America's most popular coldwater gamefish. It is comprised of 39 species in the the the following 3 subfamilies:

• **Trout, char and salmon.** Trout (6 species) are easy to distinguish from char (5 species) because trout have dark spots on a light background. Char have light spots on a dark background and prefer even colder water than trout. Like all salmonids, trout and char have a small adipose fin on the rear of their back.

Pacific salmon (5 species) differ from Atlantic salmon (1 species) in that they have a fixed life cycle. They generally return to spawn after 2 to 5 years and then die. Atlantics may live to spawn several times.

All salmon are anadromous fish, spending most of their life at sea or in the open waters of large inland lakes, and then returning to tributary streams to spawn. Some trout and char also have anadromous forms.

• **Whitefish.** This group of silvery fish (21 species) is not highly popular with anglers, but some of the larger species, such as lake whitefish and cisco, are gaining favor in parts of the North. Only one member of the group, the inconnu, is anadromous.

• **Grayling**. North America has only one species of grayling, the Arctic grayling, which is found in northern Canada, Alaska, and some pristine lakes and streams high in the Rocky Mountains of Canada and the U.S. The Arctic grayling is easily identified by its huge dorsal fin.

RAINBOW TROUT

(Oncorhynchus mykiss)

Habitat

Rainbow trout are native to the eastern Pacific and originally ascended coastal streams from northern Baja, California, to northwestern Alaska. They are also native to many inland waters west of the Rockies. The most adaptable of all trout species, the rainbow has been stocked in lakes and streams around the world.

Rainbows thrive in water from 55 to 60°F, but are able to tolerate water in the upper 70s, at least for short periods of time. They prefer fast, turbulent stretches of cool- to coldwater streams, but can survive in slow-moving sections as well. They also prosper in lakes with cold, well-oxygenated water.

Varieties

There are two distinct subspecies of rainbow trout. The red-band rainbow *(Oncorhynchus mykiss mykiss)* is the typical inland form, developing the characteristic pinkish stripe that gives the species its name. The coastal rainbow *(Oncorhynchus mykiss irideus)*, is commonly called the "steelhead" because it has a bright, silvery coloration while at sea or inhabiting the open waters of large inland lakes. Red-band rainbows, however, also develop the silvery color when stocked in

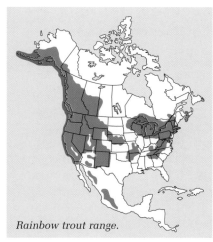

Rainbow trout range.

large lakes and are referred to as steelhead as well.

Because of the rainbow's widespread distribution and extensive stocking, more than 100 varieties of the species have evolved in North America. The Kamloops rainbow, for example, is a deep-bodied, fast-growing strain native to Kamloops Lake in British Columbia. The Skamania rainbow, native to Washington's Skamania River, is a long-bodied, broad-tailed variety that has been widely stocked in the Great Lakes.

• *Also called rainbow, bow, redsides.*

Red-band rainbows get their name from the reddish to pinkish band on their side. The coloration of the gill plates usually matches that of the lateral band. The back can be anywhere from green to blue to olive-brown, with numerous black spots. The flanks are usually silvery, the belly is white and the tail has radiating rows of black spots. Stream dwelling rainbows tend to have more intense colors and heavier spotting than lake dwellers.

Feeding Habits

Rainbows feed heavily on immature and adult insects, making them a prime target for fly fishermen and a favorite of those who favor dry flies. Rainbows also eat crustaceans, plankton and small fish, but they consume much less fish than do brown trout. As a rule, rainbows are warier and more selective about what they eat than brook trout, but not nearly as choosy as browns.

Spawning Behavior

Rainbows are spring spawners, swimming up small tributary streams to deposit their eggs. Steelhead may ascend tributary streams again in fall on what biologists call a "mock" spawning run because no egg deposition takes place.

When steelhead first enter a spawning stream, they're referred to as "bright fish," because of their bright, silvery coloration. But the longer they remain in the stream, the darker they become, eventually developing a reddish band and gill covers. The colors of the male are more intense than those of the female, and the male's lower jaw develops a pronounced hook or "kype." Steelhead feed very little while in their spawning streams.

Age/Growth

The normal life span of a rainbow is 4 to 6 years, although an occasional fish may live 10 years or more. Depending on diet and genetics, a 4-year old fish could weigh anywhere from 1 pound to 20 pounds. As a rule, stream rainbows grow much more slowly than their lake-dwelling cousins.

World Records

Landlocked rainbow: 37 pounds; Lake Pend Orielle, Idaho; November 25, 1947. *Steelhead:* 42 pounds, 2 ounces; Bell Island, Alaska; June 22, 1970.

Where to Find Rainbows

Fast-moving stretches of a trout stream are most likely to hold rainbows. Look for "pocket" water behind boulders, where trout can rest with less effort and easily dart into the current to grab drifting food.

Look for lake-dwelling rainbows around the mouths of spawning streams. They stage in these areas prior to the spawning run and then swim upriver when runoff causes the river to rise.

Typical Growth Rate

(STREAM-DWELLING RED-BAND RAINBOW)

Age	Length (inches)	Weight (pounds)
1	3.6	—
2	8.2	0.3
3	12.0	0.7
4	14.5	1.1
5	17.1	1.9
6	18.7	2.5
7	20.4	3.2
8	22.3	4.3

Steelhead resemble ordinary rainbows except that steelhead are sleeker and more silvery. The fish grow large, averaging 6 to 12 pounds. In the rushing, isolated rivers of British Columbia and Alaska, steelhead may reach weights in excess of 25 pounds.

Fishing Facts

Rainbow trout are spectacular leapers; it's not unusual for a good-sized "bow" to jump four or five times, sometimes clearing the water by several feet. Compared to most other trout species, rainbows are willing biters and can be taken on most any kind of bait or lure including spoons, spinners, plugs, flies, worms, leeches and even marshmallows. They grow to impressive sizes in remote waters; but, where fishing pressure is heavy and if catch-and-release is not practiced, the big ones are quickly removed, leaving only the smaller fish.

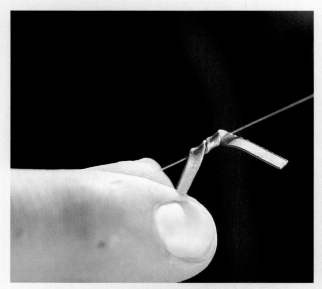

Use a twist-on leader wrap to keep your fly down in fast current. The lead strips come in a handy matchbook dispenser.

To catch steelhead in spawning streams, repeatedly drift a spawn bag, yarn fly or other egg imitation past the fish to draw a reflex strike.

Understanding Freshwater Gamefish

BROWN TROUT

(Salmo trutta)

• *Also called Loch Leven trout, German brown trout.*

Varieties

Brown trout sometimes hybridize with brook trout to produce "tiger trout," which get their

Brown trout have brownish sides that dissolve into yellow toward the belly. The sides have numerous dark spots and a few red spots, some of which have whitish to bluish halos. The adipose fin usually has a few spots, but the tail is unspotted or has only a few indistinct spots.

name from their distinctive markings (p. 112).

The anadromous form of the brown trout, called the sea trout, enter rivers along the East and West Coasts to spawn. There, they commonly reach a weight of about 5 pounds. Sea trout are also found in coastal streams of Argentina, Chile, New Zealand and Europe. The largest sea trout are caught in Argentina, Norway and Sweden, where they may reach 30 pounds.

Habitat

Found in both lakes and streams, browns can tolerate slightly warmer water than most other trout species. They prefer a water temperature in the upper 50s to low 60s and can survive for short periods of time at water temperatures near 80°F. They also seem to be more tolerant of muddy water and even some pollution.

More than any other trout, browns seek cover that offers overhead protection. During the day, the fish often hole up in the heaviest cover where it's nearly impossible to put a lure.

Browns are native to Europe and the British Isles. They have been introduced into Asia, New Zealand, North and South America and Africa. Next to rainbows, they are the most widely distributed trout in the world.

Feeding Habits

Like most other trout, browns feed heavily on aquatic insects, such as mayflies, caddisflies and stoneflies, as

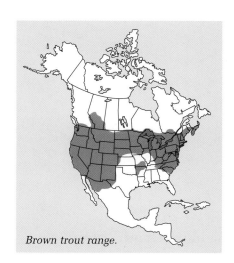

Brown trout range.

well as a variety of terrestrial forms. You may see them rising during a heavy insect hatch, but they usually base their feeding activity from a particular feeding station or lie. Unlike other trout species, you'll seldom see them cruising about at random, sipping insects off the surface.

The largest brown trout, however, are primarily fish eaters and sometimes turn cannibalistic. In fact, if a body of water has too many large browns, stocking other trout may be fruitless because they're quickly eaten. Big browns also have a liking for crayfish.

Browns tend to be nocturnal feeders, and many of the largest fish are taken after dark. In daylight hours, browns are much less likely to feed in the open than are rainbows or cutthroat.

Spawning Behavior

Brown trout are fall spawners. When the water temperature drops to the mid 40s, they begin building their redds (nests) in the upper reaches of a stream or in small tributaries. The eggs incubate over the winter and hatch in spring.

At spawning time, the yellowish coloration of the male becomes much more intense, sometimes changing to bright orange. A strong kype develops on the lower jaw and the lower fins turn charcoal-colored.

Age/Growth

Browns may live as long as 18 years, but their usual life span is 9 years or less. Their growth rate is highly variable, depending on the type of water and the food supply. In an average trout stream, the fish usually reach 18 inches by their sixth year.

Lake-dwelling brown trout, such as those in some of the Great Lakes, are much heavier for their length than stream browns. In fact, Great Lakes browns have such deep bodies that they're often called "footballs."

World Record

40 pounds, 4 ounces; Little Red River, Arkansas; May 9, 1992.

Brown Trout Varieties

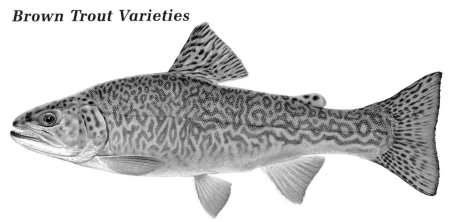

Tiger trout have a brownish to greenish background coloration with yellowish worm-like markings on the side. Because of their aggressive disposition, tiger trout are considerably easier to catch than browns.

Sea trout are pale yellow to silvery with X-shaped markings. They are sometimes confused with Atlantic salmon, because of the distinct X-shaped markings on the side. But the adipose fin of a sea trout is spotted; that of an Atlantic salmon is not.

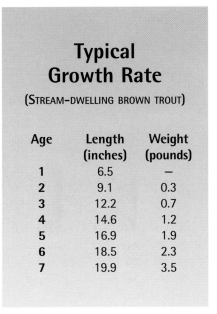

Typical Growth Rate

(STREAM–DWELLING BROWN TROUT)

Age	Length (inches)	Weight (pounds)
1	6.5	—
2	9.1	0.3
3	12.2	0.7
4	14.6	1.2
5	16.9	1.9
6	18.5	2.3
7	19.9	3.5

Fishing Facts

Many anglers consider browns the most "intelligent" trout because they can withstand heavy fishing pressure better than most other trout species. But their elusive nature is more a result of their liking for heavy cover and their night-feeding habits rather than their brainpower.

Browns will strike spinners, spoons and minnowbaits, as well as dry flies, streamers and nymphs. Good-sized minnows, nightcrawlers and other live bait account for many of the biggest browns.

Although browns are less acrobatic than rainbows, it's not unusual for them to jump once or twice when first hooked.

Look for big browns in the downstream reaches of a stream. Although these areas usually hold fewer trout, they often produce the largest fish because of the warmer water and ample supply of minnows.

Trolling with thin, bright-colored spoons produces numerous trophy browns in the Great Lakes and many other large inland lakes.

Dense, woody cover—such as logjams and brush piles—is ideal for brown trout because it offers shade and overhead protection as well as shelter from the current.

Try a big leech fly or a good-sized streamer to catch big browns. Or tie on a large, bushy dry fly that imitates a mouse or frog.

Understanding Freshwater Gamefish

CUTTHROAT TROUT

(Oncorhynchus clarki)

Varieties

Some biologists recognize more than a dozen subspecies of cutthroat trout. The most common ones include: Yellowstone cutthroat (*Oncorhynchus clarki bouvieri*), Lahontan cutthroat (*Oncorhynchus clarki henshawi*), West Slope cutthroat (*Oncorhynchus clarki lewisi*) and coastal cutthroat (*Oncorhynchus clarki clarki*). The latter, which is a sea-run form, enters streams along the Pacific coast from northern California to southwestern Alaska, usually in September and October.

Cutthroat commonly hybridize with rainbow and golden trout. Hybrids are so common in some waters that even trained biologists have a hard time making an accurate identification.

Habitat

The habitat preferences of the cutthroat are similar to those of the rainbow. They favor water temperatures from 55 to 62°F—about the same range as a rainbow. And like rainbows, cutthroats are equally at home in still or moving water, but they do not spawn successfully in a lake environment. Rainbows, however, can tolerate swifter current.

Cutthroats are quite sensitive to disruptions in their environment. The West Slope cutthroat, for example, has disappeared from all but a few of its native streams in Montana because of logging operations and stocking of rainbows. Attempts are being made to restore degraded streams so the fish can be reintroduced.

Because of the cutthroat's tendency to interbreed with rainbows and its high vulnerability to angling, it has not been widely stocked outside of its native range.

Feeding Habits

Cutthroats are highly opportunistic feeders. Most of their diet consists of insects and fish, but they also eat worms, frogs, scuds, crayfish and fish eggs.

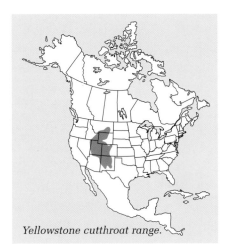

Yellowstone cutthroat range.

• *Also called cutt, red throat, native trout.*

Cutthroat trout get their name from the flaming red slash marks on the throat. Yellowstone cutthroat (above) have spots above and below the lateral line. The spots are no larger than the pupil of the eye and are more tightly grouped toward the tail.

Many anglers would argue that cutthroats are even less discriminating in their choice of food than brook trout, explaining why they're one of the easiest trout to catch. They may feed on the surface, on the bottom or anywhere in between.

Fishing Facts

Many anglers would argue that cutthroat are even easier to catch than brook trout. They are less wary than most other trout and will strike practically any kind of bait or lure that is the approximate size of their food. Cutthroat are not as acrobatic as rainbows, but a hooked fish usually wages a strong subsurface struggle.

Use a "lake troll" rig, along with a small thin metal spoon, to catch cutthroat in clear lakes. The multiple blades imitate a school of baitfish, drawing cutts to the spoon.

One of the top lures for stream cutthroats, especially coastal cutts, is a yarn fly with a single salmon egg.

Spawning Behavior

Cutthroats are spring spawners, although coastal cutthroat usually begin to spawn in late winter. Most spawning takes place in small tributary streams. An individual cutthroat may spawn only every other year.

Age/Growth

Although cutthroats may live up to 9 years, they seldom reach an age of more than 6. The growth rate is highly variable, depending mainly on subspecies and altitude. In 6 years, a West Slope cutthroat grows only to about 15 inches; a Lahontan, 24 inches.

World Record

41 pounds; Pyramid Lake, Nevada; December 19, 1925. This fish was a Lahontan cutthroat.

Typical Growth Rate
(STREAM–DWELLING FISH)

Age	Length (inches)	Weight (pounds)
1	2.1	—
2	5.5	—
3	9.2	0.5
4	12.5	1.0
5	15.8	1.8
6	19.7	3.2

Understanding Freshwater Gamefish

Other Cutthroat Subspecies

Lahontan cutthroat range.

Lahontan cutthroat are the largest cutthroat subspecies. They have widely spaced but fairly uniform spotting.

West Slope cutthroat range.

West Slope cutthroat have a spotting pattern similar to that of a Yellowstone, but there normally are no spots on the front half of the body below the lateral line.

Coastal cutthroat range.

Coastal cutthroat have silvery sides with heavy spotting. The slash marks on the throat are usually a faint pink rather than a bright red.

GOLDEN TROUT

(Oncorhynchus aguabonita)

• Also called mountain trout,
Kern River trout.

*Volcano Creek golden
trout have bright yellow sides with
a reddish lateral band that runs through about
10 dark parr marks. The sides are peppered with dark
spots, mainly above the lateral band. The dorsal, anal and
pelvic fins have white tips and the tail is spotted.*

Varieties

Although there is some dis-
agreement on the taxonomy
of golden trout, most experts
recognize two subspecies: the
Volcano Creek golden trout
(*Oncorhynchus aguabonita
aguabonita*) and the Little
Kern golden trout
(*Oncorhynchus aguabonita
whitei*). Golden trout commonly hybridize with rainbows and, on occasion, with
cutthroats.

Habitat

Goldens are most common
in lakes and streams in

mountainous areas of the
West. They were originally
found only at high altitudes
(above 6,000 feet), but they
have been stocked at lower
elevations where they seem to
do equally well. Golden trout
prefer a water temperature in
the upper 50s to low 60s but
can tolerate temperatures into
the low 70s.

Feeding Habits

Insects and small crus-
taceans comprise most of the
diet. Golden trout are sporadic feeders, often gorging
themselves for a day or two

Golden trout range.

and then barely feeding at all
for several days.

Spawning Behavior

Spawning takes place in
early- to mid-summer when
the water temperature reaches
about 50°F. A female digs several redds, usually in the tail
of a pool in the stream channel or in a tributary. Lake-
dwelling fish may spawn successfully in inlet or outlet
streams.

Age/Growth

These slow-growing fish
seldom reach the size of rainbows, browns or cutts. Their

*Little Kern golden trout resemble Volcano Creek goldens, but they
have black spots mainly near the tail.*

Typical Growth Rate

Age	Length (inches)	Weight (pounds)
1	3.5	—
2	5.5	—
3	8.0	0.2
4	10.1	0.4
5	11.7	0.7
6	13.2	1.0

life span in most waters is about 7 years, and it is rare for them to reach a weight of more than 1 pound in that time.

World Record

11 pounds; Cook's Lake, Wyoming; August 5, 1948.

Fishing Facts

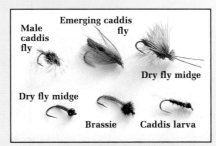

Golden trout are particularly fond of tiny midge and caddisfly imitations, because these insects comprise a large part of their diet.

There are times when goldens will take absolutely nothing other than a fly that precisely imitates their food. But more often, they boil at most any kind of lure or bait you toss into the water.

The largest golden trout are taken from remote waters at high altitudes (10,000 feet or more). There, the only access is by hiking, and the fish have a better chance of long-term survival.

Look for golden trout in alpine lakes in the West. Because these lakes are at such a high altitude, they do not necessarily have to be deep to have water cold enough for goldens.

BROOK TROUT

(Salvelinus fontinalis)

• Also called Eastern brook trout, speckled trout, squaretail and brookie.

Brook trout have light-colored spots on a darker background and white leading edges on the lower fins. The back is covered with pale, worm-like markings and the sides have a few small reddish spots with bluish halos. The brook trout's tail is not as deeply forked as that of other chars, explaining why the fish are sometimes called "squaretails."

Varieties

Hybrids called "splake" are produced in hatcheries by crossing male brook trout with female lake trout. Splake can be identified by their tail, which is forked more than that of a brook trout, but less than that of a lake trout (see p. 124). The "tiger trout," which has worm-like markings over the entire side, is a cross between a brook trout and a brown trout (see p. 112).

"Coasters" are to brook trout what "steelhead" are to rainbow trout. Although they are quite rare, coasters can still be found in parts of the Great Lakes, particularly lakes Superior and Michigan.

Habitat

Like other chars, brook trout require cold, clear water. They favor water in the range of 52 to 56°F and are seldom found at temperatures above 68°F. Their need for frigid water explains why they are often found in the headwaters of streams, where the spring flow is highest and water temperatures, coldest. Brook trout are commonly stocked in coldwater lakes, but only in rare cases do they reproduce in still water.

Native to most of northeastern North America and the Appalachian Mountains as far south as Georgia, brook trout have been widely stocked in the western United States and Canada. They have also been planted in parts of South America, New Zealand, Europe and Asia.

Feeding Habits

Brook trout are known for their voracious, non-selective feeding habits. Small- to medium-sized brook trout feed mainly on immature aquatic insects and terrestrial insects. But as the fish grow larger, their diet broadens to include

Brook trout range.

worms, leeches, crustaceans, salamanders, fish, small mammals and even snakes.

Spawning Behavior

Brook trout are fall spawners. When water temperatures dip into the 40s, the females begin digging redds in gravel beds in the headwaters of the stream or in gravelly tributaries. After the eggs are deposited and fertilized, they are covered with gravel and left to incubate until the following spring.

Age/Growth

Brook trout grow relatively slowly and are prone to stunting. Because of their preference for cold water, the fish grow fastest in the northern part of their range. They have been known to live up to 15 years.

World Record

14 pounds, 8 ounces; Nipigon River, Ontario; July, 1916.

Typical Growth Rate

Age	Length (inches)	Weight (pounds)
1	6.2	0.1
2	7.7	0.2
3	9.0	0.4
4	10.5	0.6
5	12.4	0.9
6	13.8	1.3
7	15.0	1.7

A male brook trout in spawning colors is arguably the most beautiful of all trout.

Fishing Facts

The brook trout's gluttonous feeding habits, combined with its lack of wariness, explain why it is one of the easiest trout to catch on hook and line. Although brookies are scrappy fighters, they don't display the aerial antics of a rainbow. Fish connoisseurs rate brook trout near the top of the table-quality list. Their firm white to pink-tinted meat has a sweet, delicate flavor.

Look for brook trout in newly-created beaver ponds on small streams. Although the fish may be stunted in free-flowing portions of the stream, they grow much larger in the beaver ponds because of the warmer water and plentiful supply of food. Older ponds, however, are usually too silty for good food production.

On most good-sized streams, you're most likely to find brook trout in headwaters areas with good spring flow. Farther downstream, the water often becomes too warm for brookies.

Understanding Freshwater Gamefish

LAKE TROUT

(Salvelinus namaycush)

• *Also called laker, gray trout, mackinaw, togue.*

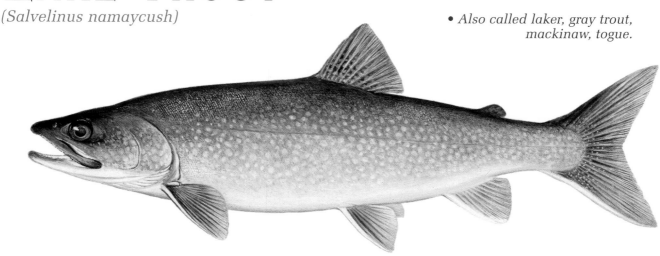

Lake trout have light spots on a greenish to grayish background, and a deeply-forked tail. The lower fins have white leading edges. Lean trout (shown) have a longer, leaner body than the siscowet (below), and the fat content of the flesh is less than 50 percent.

Varieties

Taxonomists have identified numerous "races" of lake trout, but only two distinct subspecies: the lean trout (*Salvelinus namaycush namaycush*) and the fat trout or "siscowet" (*Salvelinus namaycush siscowet*), which is found only in Lake Superior.

Male brook trout can be crossed with female lake trout to produce "splake" (speckled trout x lake trout, p. 124). These fish are sometimes stocked in infertile northern lakes. On occasion, lake trout also cross with Arctic char.

Habitat

The lake trout's preferred temperature range is 48 to 52°F, lower than that of any other freshwater gamefish.

Lake trout range.

This explains why they are found primarily in deep, infertile lakes. Fertile lakes, even if they were deep, would not have adequate dissolved oxygen in the depths.

Lake trout commonly inhabit depths of 50 to 125

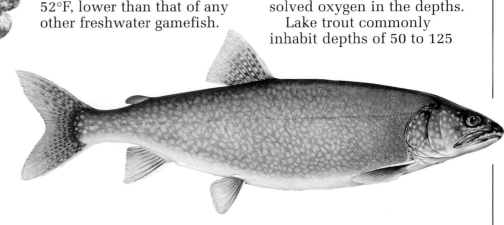

The body of a siscowet is deeper than that of a lean trout and the fat content of the flesh may be as high as 80 percent.

feet and may be considerably deeper. But lakers are not always found in such deep water. In very large lakes, such as Lake Superior, they're frequently caught on the surface, even in summer, because the surface temperature is within their comfort zone.

Feeding Habits

In most waters, the lake trout's diet consists mainly of fish. They commonly eat coldwater species such as ciscoes, whitefish, smelt and burbot, but they will take whatever is available. In lakes where forage fish are scarce, lakers feed on plankton, crustaceans and insects. But in this situation they rarely grow larger than 2 or 3 pounds.

The feeding habits of lake trout are unusual in that the fish can move up and down considerable distances in the water column to find food. A laker in 80 feet of water, for instance, can easily swim up 50 feet to take ciscoes suspended in the thermocline. They compensate for water pressure changes by burping up air through a duct connecting their swim bladder to their esophagus.

Spawning Behavior

Lakers spawn in the fall, usually at water temperatures in the upper 40s or low 50s. They deposit their eggs on rocky reefs from a few feet to more than 30 feet deep. The eggs fall into crevices in the rocks, where they can incubate safe from predators and then hatch in spring. Lake trout spawn on the same reefs each year.

Age/Growth

Lake trout grow very slowly. But they may live as long as 40 years. Typically, it takes about 11 years for a lake trout to reach 5 pounds and, in the Far North where the growing season is extremely short, it may take twice that long.

Nevertheless, lake trout reach astonishing sizes. In northern Canada and a few large lakes in the western states, 30- to 40-pound lakers are fairly common and anglers take an occasional giant exceeding 50 pounds. The biggest lake trout on record was netted in Saskatchewan's Lake Athabasca. It weighed 102 pounds.

World Record

72 pounds, 4 ounces; Great Bear Lake, Northwest Territories; August 19, 1995.

Typical Growth Rate

Age	Length (inches)	Weight (pounds)
1	4.1	–
3	8.7	.3
5	13.3	1.0
7	17.9	2.1
9	21.9	3.9
11	25.2	5.7
13	29.8	12.1
15	33.2	15.0
17	36.8	19.4
19	38.9	25.1

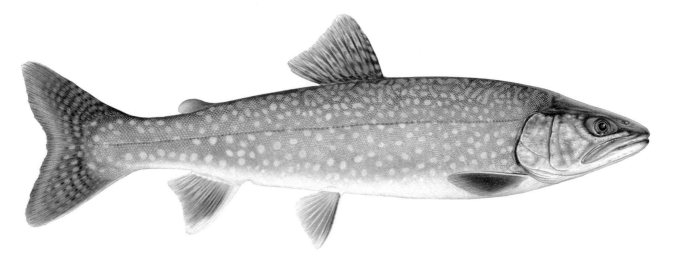

Splake resemble lake trout, but they have the brook trout's worm-like markings on the back, and the tail is not as deeply forked. The world record splake weighed 20 pounds, 11 ounces. It was taken in Georgian Bay, Ontario, on May 17, 1987.

Understanding Freshwater Gamefish

Fishing Facts

How you fish lake trout depends mainly on how deep they are. In spring and fall, when they're shallow, try casting or long-line trolling with spoons or plugs, or still-fishing with dead bait such as a smelt, cisco or chunk of sucker meat.

When they go deep in summer, you can reach them with downriggers, by deep-trolling with 3-way swivel rigs or by vertically jigging.

Lake trout stay active all winter and are relatively easy to catch by ice fishing. And they're found in pretty much the same areas where you would find them in summer.

Because lake trout grow so slowly, fishing regulations must be quite restrictive to prevent overharvest. Bag limits are generally low and open seasons short.

Vertically jigging with a bladebait makes it possible to catch lake trout in deep water without resorting to wire line, downriggers or other heavy tackle.

Try an airplane jig tipped with a minnow or cut bait to catch lakers through the ice. An airplane jig swims in wide circles, covering more water than most other lures.

When lake trout are tightly schooled in deep water, just drop a heavy spoon (1 ounce or more) to the bottom and rapidly reel it back up. The fish may hit at any depth.

Because lake trout grow so slowly, it's important to release any large lake trout that you catch to ensure quality fishing in the future.

BULL TROUT

(Salvelinus confluentus)

• *Also called bull char.*

Bull trout have bright orange to pinkish to whitish spots on an olive background. The lower fins have white leading edges. The long, broad, flattened head gives the bull trout a distinctive look.

Close Relatives

Bull trout are sometimes mistaken for lake trout, but their spots are usually pink or orange rather than white and their tail is not as forked. They are also easily confused with Dolly Varden. In fact, the two were once considered the same species, but the head of a bull trout is much flatter and wider than that of a Dolly.

Habitat

Bull trout are actually char, so they prefer colder water than most other trout species, generally in the 45 to 55°F range. Primarily lake-dwellers, bull trout inhabit deep, cold, infertile lakes like those that commonly hold lake trout. But they're also found in good-sized trout streams.

Feeding Habits

Fish (including trout) make up the bulk of a bull trout's diet. But bulls don't hesitate to take crayfish, clams, snails and immature aquatic insects.

Spawning Behavior

Bull trout spawn in early fall, but they often begin their upstream migration in late spring or early summer. Both lake- and stream-dwelling bulls require moving water to spawn successfully. They generally build their redds in small tributaries of the main river, usually when the water temperature is 45 to 50°F. It's not unusual for bulls to swim more than 50 miles to reach their spawning grounds.

Age/Growth

Bull trout have been known to live up to 20 years. Although they grow slowly in their first few years of life, their growth rate speeds up once they begin to feed on fish. A 10-year-old bull usually weighs 10 to 12 pounds.

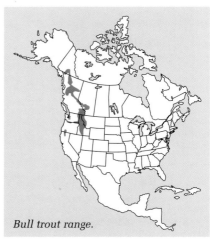

Bull trout range.

Typical Growth Rate

Age	Length (inches)	Weight (pounds)
1	3.0	–
2	5.4	–
3	8.1	0.2
4	12.3	0.6
5	17.5	1.8
6	22.4	3.7
7	25.8	6.0
8	28.2	8.9
9	30.0	11.2

World Record

32 pounds; Lake Pend Orielle, Idaho; October 27, 1949.

Fishing Facts

Bull trout have gained a reputation as being serious predators on other trout species. Their fish-eating habits, combined with their reluctance to take a fly, explains why they aren't as popular as most other trout species.

Some anglers, however, regard the bull trout as a true trophy. Bulls are extremely tough fighters, waging a stubborn battle in deep water. They sometimes grow to a weight of more than 20 pounds.

Look for the stream's deepest pools to find bull trout. Fish on the bottom using a live-bait rig or a deep-running artificial.

DOLLY VARDEN

(Salvelinus malma)

• *Also called Dolly, red-spotted char.*

Dolly Varden resemble Arctic char, but the spots are usually smaller. Typically, the largest spots are smaller than the pupil of the eye. The lower fins have white leading edges. Sea-run Dollies (above) have silvery sides with pinkish spots. They grow much larger than landlocks, but seldom exceed 8 pounds.

This colorful char supposedly got its name from a Charles Dickens book, Barnaby Rudge, in which one of the characters, Miss Dolly Varden, wore a pink-spotted dress and hat.

Varieties/Close Relatives

Although there are no officially recognized subspecies, there are two distinct forms of Dolly Varden: sea-run and landlocked.

Sea-run Dollies can easily be confused with Arctic char (p. 130); in fact, some taxonomists believe they are the same species. But char normally have larger spots than Dollies.

Habitat

Sea-run Dolly Varden are found from northern California up the Pacific Coast to Alaska and around the northern Pacific Rim from Japan to Korea and in some Siberian waters. Landlocked Dollies inhabit many coldwater lakes and streams in the West. The Dolly's preferred temperature range is 50 to 55°F.

Feeding Habits

Dollies feed mainly on small fish, fish eggs, snails and insects. Although Dollies do eat salmon eggs, they are usually dead eggs that have drifted from the redds.

Dolly Varden range.

Spawning Behavior

Dollies are fall spawners, building their redds in the main channel of a good-sized stream when the water temperature drops into the low to mid 40s. More than half of the fish die after spawning has been completed.

Age/Growth

Dollies grow fastest in the northern part of their range, reaching about 5 pounds in

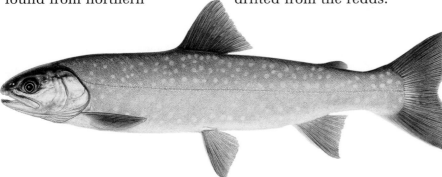

Landlocked Dollies have silvery-green sides with pinkish spots, but the color of the spots is more intense than those of sea-runs. Landlocks rarely grow larger than 3 pounds.

Fishing Facts

The Dolly's habit of eating salmon eggs and sometimes young salmon does little for its popularity among West Coast anglers. But the lack of respect is unwarranted because most of the eggs they eat are already dead. Dollies (particularly small ones) sometimes feed on insects and can readily be taken on dry flies. Larger ones are more easily caught on spinners, spoons, plugs, streamers or live bait, especially salmon eggs.

To fish a single salmon egg, rig it on a size 10 to 14 salmon-egg hook, which has an extra-short shank and a turned-up eye. First, push the hook through the side of the egg (1), then turn the hook 180 degrees (2) and bury the point in the opposite side of the egg.

10 years. In the southern part, they grow to only half that size in the same period. The fish may live up to 19 years.

World Record

18 pounds, 9 ounces; Mashutuk River, Alaska; July 13, 1993.

Typical Growth Rate

Age	Length (inches)	Weight (pounds)
1	3.6	–
2	6.3	–
3	9.0	0.3
4	11.6	0.5
5	13.9	0.8
6	15.5	1.3
7	17.1	1.6
8	18.8	1.9
9	20.0	2.1

ARCTIC CHAR

(Salvelinus alpinus)

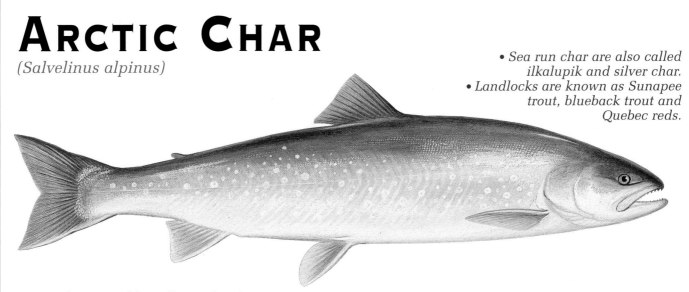

Arctic char resemble Dolly Varden, but the spots are larger, the largest ones being at least the size of the pupil of the eye. Sea-run char (above) are silvery with pinkish spots when they first move into their spawning stream, but the color intensifies greatly as spawning time approaches. The spots turn a brilliant red, as do the flanks and lower fins, and the lower jaw of the male develops a slight kype.

Arctic char range.

Varieties/Close Relatives

Like the closely related Dolly Varden (p. 128), the Arctic char has two distinct forms: Sea-run and land-locked.

Habitat

Arctic char are found in cold waters of the northern hemisphere, ranging from Alaska and northern Canada to Baffin Island, Greenland, Iceland, northern Norway and northern Siberia.

Landlocked Arctic char inhabit the deep, cold infertile lakes of southern Quebec, south-west Alaska and northern New England, where they are often called "Sunapee" trout. Landlocks are also found in Norway, Sweden, Finland, England, Ireland, Scotland, west-central Europe and Russia.

Unlike steelhead and salmon, sea-run char seldom range far from the mouth of their home stream.

Feeding Habits

Arctic char are not fussy feeders. They will eat whatever they can find, including plankton, eels, small fish, crustaceans and insects.

Spawning Behavior

Sea-run char begin their upstream migration in late summer, spawning in slow-moving pools when the water temperature drops into the low 40s or upper 30s. After spawning, the fish remain in the stream, overwintering in deep pools or connecting lakes, then returning to the sea in spring.

Landlocked char spawn on rocky main-lake reefs or in tributary streams.

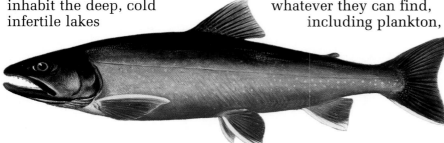

Landlocked char have greenish to grayish sides with spots that range from reddish to pinkish to off-white.

Fishing Facts

The Arctic char's willingness to take a wide variety of foods explains why it is one of the easiest salmonids to catch on hook and line. The fish are easily taken on streamers and will sometimes rise to dry flies, but most anglers rely on flashy spoons.

Sea-run char are formidable fish, reaching weights of 25 pounds and waging a powerful fight when hooked. It's not unusual for one to catapult from the water several times. But the fish "lose steam" after they've been in the stream for a long period of time.

Large numbers of Arctic char overwinter in tundra lakes where native anglers ice-fish for them using primitive gear—usually a short stick and a spoon tied to a heavy string.

Heavy casting spoons are ideal for catching char because you can cast them a long distance and they stay down in the current.

Age/Growth

Although Arctic char grow very slowly, they may live up to 40 years. Sea-run fish grow considerably faster and reach a much larger size than landlocks.

World Record

32 pounds, 9 ounces; Tree River, Northwest Territories; July 30, 1981.

Typical Growth Rate

(HUDSON BAY SEA-RUN)

Age	Length (inches)	Weight (pounds)
4	14.4	1.3
6	17.1	2.1
8	19.7	3.4
10	22.0	5.2
12	25.3	7.2
14	26.7	8.4
16	28.5	10.1
18	31.5	13.4
22	34.6	16.2

Understanding Freshwater Gamefish

CHINOOK SALMON

(Oncorhynchus tshawytscha)

• *Also called king salmon, quinnat, tyee, blackjaw, blackmouth.*

Because they reach such massive size, chinooks are often called "king" salmon. In 1949, a mammoth 126-pounder was caught in a fish trap near Petersburg, Alaska.

Sea-run chinook salmon have silvery sides and an iridescent greenish to blue-green back. The upper half of the body has numerous black spots. Chinooks resemble cohos, but the anal fin is longer, both lobes of the tail are spotted, and the gums are blackish (p. 134).

Chinook salmon range.

Varieties

Chinook salmon sometimes hybridize with coho salmon.

Habitat

After completing their life at sea, chinooks migrate up large rivers along the Pacific coast to spawn. Chinooks are stocked in the Great Lakes, the Missouri River reservoirs and many other smaller inland lakes. They prefer

water temperatures from 53 to 57°F.

Feeding Habits

The diet of sea-run chinooks consists mainly of fish, particularly herring and sand lance, but they also eat squid, shrimp and other crustaceans. In the Great Lakes, chinooks feed mainly on alewives, smelt and chubs.

Spawning Behavior

Some chinooks enter their spawning streams early in the season, while others wait until much later, explaining why anglers commonly refer to "spring" chinooks and "fall" chinooks. Spring chinooks spawn in early fall; fall chinooks, in late fall. Water temperatures at spawning time vary from 40 to 55°F. Because chinooks are

Spawning chinooks have reddish to copper-colored sides. Males develop a hooked upper jaw, a distinct kype and large canine teeth. The color of the female is less intense.

powerful swimmers with the ability to leap over seemingly impassible barriers, they can swim incredible distances upstream to spawn, often more than 1,000 miles. When they reach their spawning grounds, the female digs one or more large redds (up to 12 feet long) in coarse gravel. After spawning, she guards the eggs but usually dies within several days.

Age/Growth

Although chinooks may return to spawn as early as age 2 or as late as age 9, the majority return at age 4. Then they normally weigh 20 to 30 pounds, although fish in cer-tain streams may reach twice or even three times that size. Males grow faster than females, and Alaskan chinooks reach considerably larger sizes than Great Lakes chinooks.

World Record

97 pounds, 4 ounces; Kenai River, Alaska; May 17, 1985.

Chinook vs. Coho

On a chinook salmon (left), the teeth protrude from blackish gums, and the lower jaw is sharply pointed. On a coho (right), the teeth protrude from grayish or whitish gums, and the jaw is not as sharply pointed.

Typical Growth Rate
(SEA-RUN CHINOOK)

Age	Length (inches)	Weight (pounds)
1	3.4	—
2	16.5	1.5
3	27.1	8.6
4	35.6	20.9
5	42.0	35.0
6	45.8	45.4

Where to Find Chinooks

In coastal streams, especially those fed by milky glacial meltwater, look for chinooks at the mouth of a clear-water tributary. The fish often hold along the seam between the clear and discolored water.

Great Lakes kings often congregate in deep water off steep cliffs in summer. You can also find them along the edges of deep reefs and breaklines several miles away from shore.

Fishing Facts

King salmon are incredibly strong fighters. A fisherman once fought a giant Alaskan king for more than 24 hours before losing it at the net. It's not unusual for a king to run off 200 yards of line, and anglers have reported chasing the fish for more than a mile!

There are many ways to catch king salmon. In early season, when kings are still in saltwater, you can troll for them with herring rigs around the mouths of spawning streams. Later in the season, you can troll or cast with spoons, spinners and plugs or drift with fresh spawn.

Great Lakes fishermen usually troll artificials in open water using downriggers.

Kings are rated slightly below sockeye and coho salmon on the table-quality scale, but their reddish-orange flesh is still very good.

Trolling plugs with a scooped-out face, such as the Luhr Jensen J-Plug, have an erratic action that appeals to chinook salmon. These lures work best when trolled at high speeds.

When kings enter their spawning streams, try drifting a Spin-n-Glo tipped with fresh spawn through a deep pool or run. The combination of flash and scent is hard for kings to resist.

Heavy spinners are a good choice for fishing in swift current. To keep the lure on the bottom where kings are normally found, cast it and then let it sink on a slack line for few seconds before starting a slow retrieve.

Great Lakes anglers commonly troll for kings using trolling spoons or plugs on downriggers. Not only do downriggers enable you to precisely control your depth, they make it possible to spread lines at various levels.

COHO SALMON
(Oncorhynchus kisutch)

• *Also called silver salmon.*

Sea-run coho salmon have bright silvery sides with a metallic bluish or greenish back. The upper half of the body has numerous black spots. Cohos resemble chinooks, but the anal fin is shorter and the teeth protrude from whitish or grayish, rather than blackish gums (p. 134).

Varieties

Coho salmon occasionally hybridize with chinook salmon.

Habitat

After spending most of their life at sea, cohos move into rivers and streams along the Pacific coast to spawn. Cohos have been stocked in many inland waters, including the Great Lakes, prairie reservoirs on the Missouri River and numerous smaller lakes in the West. Cohos prefer water temperatures in the 53 to 57°F range.

Feeding Habits

Small fish, including herring and pilchard, make up most of the coho's diet. They also eat zooplankton, small crustaceans and the young of other kinds of salmon. Great Lakes coho feed mainly on alewives and smelt.

Spawning Behavior

Coho spawn later than other Pacific salmon, usually in mid to late fall at water temperatures in the mid 40s to low 50s. And they migrate farther upstream than any other salmon, with the exception of the chinook. The female excavates a large redd on a gravelly bottom in swift water. She guards the nest for several days after spawning and then dies.

Age/Growth

Cohos return to spawn at 2 to 5 years of age,

Coho salmon range.

but the majority spawn at age 3. At that time, they usually weigh from 6 to 10 pounds. Males grow more rapidly than females.

World Record

33 pounds, 7 ounces; Lake Ontario; August 13, 1998.

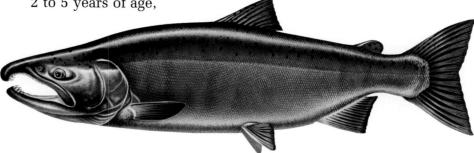

Spawning coho salmon have pinkish to reddish sides and a greenish head. The male (shown) has a strongly hooked upper jaw, a distinct kype and large canine teeth.

Typical Growth Rate

(SEA-RUN COHO)

Age	Length (inches)	Weight (pounds)
1	5.6	—
2	13.6	1.0
3	27.5	7.4
4	30.0	11.4
5	32.6	14.8

Fishing Facts

The aggressive nature and spectacular leaping ability of the coho make it a favorite among open-water trollers and stream fishermen. Cohos will take a variety of artificials including spoons, spinners plugs and flies. They can also be caught on spawn bags, shrimp and herring rigs. Cohos have flame red flesh that is comparable to that of the sockeye.

Coho in open water often favor small lures, such as a trolling fly fished behind a dodger. Experiment with different leader lengths. A 12-inch leader gives the fly a fast, darting action; a 20-inch, a slower swimming motion.

For stream fishing, use a heavy spoon that will get down in fast current. Cohos seem to prefer a silver spoon with a touch of chartreuse or green.

PINK SALMON

(Oncorhynchus gorbuscha)

• *Also called humpback salmon, humpy, autumn salmon.*

The name "pink" salmon is derived from the color of the flesh after it has been canned.

Sea-run pink salmon have silvery sides and a steel-blue to blue-green back. The upper part of the body, the adipose fin and the entire tail have large black spots, some of which are the size of the eye.

Varieties

On occasion, pink salmon hybridize with chum salmon.

Habitat

Pink salmon spend their adult life at sea and then migrate up Pacific coastal streams to spawn. In the 1950s, pinks were released into Lake Superior and have since become established in all of the Great Lakes. Pinks prefer water temperatures in the 52 to 57°F range.

Feeding Habits

Pink salmon feed mainly on zooplankton, small fish, crustaceans, squid and molluscs. After entering their spawning streams, they do not feed.

Spawning Behavior

Spawning takes place from late summer to late fall, usu-ally at water temperatures from 43 to 48°F. Pinks seldom migrate more than 40 miles upstream to reach their spawning grounds, and some may spawn in the intertidal zone. Females dig redds in gravelly riffles only 1 to 2 feet deep, while males use their large canine teeth to vigorous-ly defend their territory. After spawning, females guard the nests for as long as they can but usually die within a week.

Age/Growth

An occasional pink may live 3 years, but the vast majority live only 2. This explains why spawning runs are usually heavier in alter-nate years. In their 2-year life span, they generally reach a weight of 3 to 6 pounds. Great Lakes pinks are consid-erably smaller, seldom exceeding 2 pounds. Males grow faster than females.

Pink salmon range.

World Record

12 pounds, 9 ounces; con-fluence of Moose and Kenai rivers, Alaska; August 17, 1974.

Typical Growth Rate

Age	Length (inches)	Weight (pounds)
1	13.1	0.9
2	23.9	4.1
3	27.4	8.0

Fishing Facts

Pink salmon present a challenge to anglers. Even though a stream is teeming with fish, they may be difficult to catch because they are not feeding. Another problem: The fish deteriorate quickly once in the stream, so the fish you catch may not be fit to eat. If you can intercept the fish in the lower reaches of the stream or in intertidal areas, however, you can enjoy some fast action for pinks that are still in good condition.

Fish intertidal areas of coastal streams on an incoming tide, which tends to bring in pinks. The "bright" fish are more likely to strike lures than are fish that have been in the stream for several days or weeks.

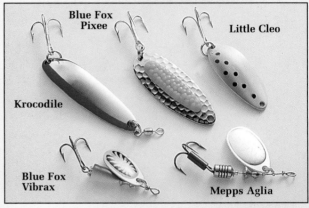

Small spinners and spoons account for the majority of pink salmon. Retrieve the lure slowly, keeping it just a few inches off the bottom.

A spawning male humpy has a grotesque look.

Understanding Freshwater Gamefish

SOCKEYE SALMON

(Oncorhynchus nerka)

• *Also called red salmon, blueback salmon.*

Sockeye salmon range.

Sea-run sockeye salmon are silvery with a metallic-blue or blue-green coloration on the back and top of the head. There are no distinct black spots on the back or tail although the back may have a few dark speckles. Sea-run sockeyes resemble chum salmon, but their jaw is shorter, extending only to the rear of the eye.

Varieties

The landlocked form of the sockeye salmon is called the kokanee (below).

Habitat

Sockeyes are anadromous, spending most of their life at sea and then returning to spawn in Pacific coastal streams, usually those flowing out of inland lakes. Kokanee have been stocked in many deep, cold lakes in the western states. The sockeye's preferred temperature range is 50 to 55°F.

Feeding Habits

Sea-run sockeyes feed mainly on zooplankton and crustaceans. They seldom eat fish. Kokanee are also plankton eaters, but they feed on immature aquatic insects as well.

Spawning Behavior

In late summer or early fall, when the water temperature is in the mid 40s to low 50s, sockeyes migrate upriver. They may spawn below the outlet of a lake or swim into the lake and spawn in tributary streams. The female digs several redds and after the eggs are deposited, both parents guard the redds as long as their strength allows.

Age/Growth

Sockeyes return to spawn at 3 to 8 years of age, but the majority return at age 4. They die several days after spawning. Male sockeyes grow faster than females. Sea-run sockeyes seldom exceed 10 pounds; kokanees, 2 pounds.

World Records

Sea-run: 13 pounds, 9 ounces; Kenai River, Alaska; July 26, 1992.
Kokanee: 9 pounds, 6 ounces; Okanagan Lake, British Columbia; June 18, 1988.

Kokanee resemble sea-run sockeyes, but they are considerably smaller with a slimmer body.

Spawning sockeyes are brilliant red with a parrot-green head. The male (shown) develops a long, hooked upper jaw, a prominent kype and a noticeable hump just behind the head.

Where to Find Sockeyes and Kokanees

Look for spawning sockeyes just below the outlet (arrow) of a lake that feeds a major spawning stream. Or, try tributary streams that flow into the lake.

Kokanee are found mainly in deep, cold, infertile lakes in the western U.S. and Canada.

Typical Growth Rate

(SEA-RUN SOCKEYE)

Age	Length (inches)	Weight (pounds)
1	3.5*	—
2	4.8*	—
3	22.4	3.9
4	25.6	6.0
5	27.8	7.7

* Juvenile fish living in streams before going to sea

Fishing Facts

Fish connoisseurs rate sockeye salmon near the top of the table-quality list. The flame-red flesh has a delicate flavor and commands a higher price than any other salmon.

Sockeyes are great sport fish as well; their aerial acrobatics are equal to those of the coho. But sockeyes can be a challenge to catch. Because their diet consists mainly of plankton and other tiny food items, they seldom strike large lures. They can be caught on a single salmon egg or piece of worm, and fly fishermen often have good success on flies, particularly sparsely tied streamers. Kokanee are often taken on a piece of worm behind "cowbells."

Look for sockeyes in relatively fast, broken current. Although the fish will hold in fairly still water, they are much spookier and may be almost impossible to catch.

Use a bright-colored, sparsely tied streamer to catch spawning sockeyes. Bulky flies or those tied with drab-colored materials seldom work as well.

When trolling for kokanees, use "cowbells" or "pop gear" ahead of a Flutterspoon or a hook baited with a piece of worm. The large spinner blades can easily be seen from a distance.

Jig for kokanees through the ice using a small jigging lure, such as a size 3 Swedish pimple. Tip it with a kernel of white corn or a grub.

CHUM SALMON
(Oncorhynchus keta)

• *Also called dog salmon, calico salmon, autumn salmon.*

Sea-run chum salmon have silvery sides, sometimes with faint vertical bars. The back is bluish, and there are no distinct spots on the back or tail. Chum salmon resemble sockeyes, but the chum's jaw is longer, extending past the rear of the eye.

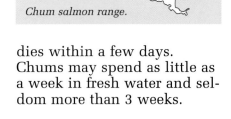

Chum salmon range.

Varieties

Chum salmon occasionally hybridize with pink salmon.

Habitat

Although chum salmon are anadromous, they do not have the leaping ability of other Pacific salmon, so they cannot negotiate steep waterfalls or other serious obstacles. They seldom migrate more than 100 miles upstream. Chum salmon prefer water temperatures in the 54 to 57°F range.

Feeding Habits

The chum salmon's diet consists of zooplankton, small fish, crustaceans and squid. Once they enter their spawning streams, they are at an advanced state of sexual maturity, so they do not feed.

Spawning Behavior

Chum salmon begin their spawning migration in late summer or early fall, usually when water temperatures are in the mid 40s to mid 50s. The female digs one or more redds on a gravelly or rocky bottom. After spawning, she guards the redds but usually dies within a few days. Chums may spend as little as a week in fresh water and seldom more than 3 weeks.

Spawning chum salmon have greenish sides with distinctive purple bands and white tips on the anal and pelvic fins. The male (shown) has a hooked upper jaw, a moderate kype and large canine teeth.

Age/Growth

Although chum salmon may return to spawn as early as age 2 or as late as age 7, the majority return at age 4. At that time they usually weigh from 5 to 10 pounds, depending on the stream. Males generally grow faster than females.

World Record

32 pounds; Edye Pass, British Columbia; July 11, 1995.

Typical Growth Rate

Age	Length (inches)	Weight (pounds)
1	7.9	—
2	16.2	2.1
3	22.4	5.0
4	27.9	9.9
5	31.5	14.7

Fishing Facts

Because chum salmon do not have the flame-red flesh of the sockeye, coho or chinook, their table quality is considered inferior. In fact, Eskimos and trappers sometimes feed them to their dogs, explaining the common name "dog salmon." But chums are strong fighters and are commonly caught on spinners and small spoons.

Look for chum salmon in deep pools; they usually hold at the downstream end or "tail" of a pool (arrow). Although you won't be able to see them, these fish are much more catchable than are visible fish in clear, shallow water.

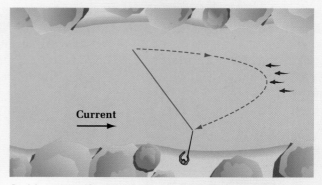

Current

Position yourself a little upstream from the fish and then angle your cast across stream. Try to time your retrieve so the lure changes direction and begins heading upstream just as it reaches the fish.

ATLANTIC SALMON

(Salmo salar)

• *Landlocked form also called Sebago salmon, Ouananiche, landlock.*

Sea-run Atlantic salmon have silvery sides and a steel-blue back. The upper half of the body has small X-shaped black spots, but the tail is unspotted.

Atlantic salmon range.

Varieties

Although no subspecies are recognized, there are two distinct varieties of Atlantic salmon—the sea-run or anadromous form and the landlocked form. Several strains of landlocks have been identified, the most common being the Ouananiche and Sebago salmon.

Habitat

Atlantic salmon are native to the North Atlantic region. Anadromous Atlantic salmon enter cold, clear streams along the North Atlantic seaboard, particularly in Newfoundland, Labrador and Quebec.

Landlocks are found in clear, cold lakes that have gravel-bottomed inlets suitable for spawning. The Atlantic's preferred temperature range is 53 to 59°F.

Feeding Habits

The diet consists mainly of small crustaceans and fish. Sand lance and herring are important foods for sea-run Atlantics; smelt, for landlocks.

Spawning Behavior

Atlantics may move into their spawning streams from spring to early fall. They swim long distances upstream and have the astounding ability to negotiate tremendous waterfalls to reach their spawning grounds. In late fall, at water temperatures from the low 40s to about 50, the female digs one or more large redds, usually in riffle areas. She abandons the eggs after spawning and may return to the sea, but the male usually remains in the river, sometimes through the winter.

Landlocks spawn in riffle areas of inlet streams.

Spawning Atlantic salmon, with their yellowish to brownish sides and orange spots, resemble brown trout. But the adipose fin, unlike that of a brown, is unspotted. Males (shown) develop a noticeable kype.

Landlocked Atlantic salmon have silvery sides with a brownish or bluish cast. Their spots are bigger than those of a sea-run, and may have light-colored halos.

Typical Growth Rate

(SEA-RUN ATLANTIC SALMON)

Age	Length (inches)	Weight (pounds)
3	22.0	4.2
4	30.5	10.2
5	35.2	17.6
6	39.8	26.0
7	42.5	33.2

Age/Growth

Atlantics may live up to 10 years, spending their first 2 or 3 years in the stream before migrating to sea or to a lake. Sea-run Atlantics commonly reach weights of 30 pounds; landlocks rarely exceed 5 pounds. Males grow more rapidly than females.

World Records

Sea-run: 79 pounds, 2 ounces; Tana River, Norway; 1928.

Landlocked: 22 pounds, 11 ounces; Lobstick Lake, Newfoundland; August 24, 1982.

Fishing Facts

Atlantic salmon are the ultimate gamefish. Their leaping ability is legendary and, even though they do not feed once they enter their spawning streams, they readily take flies, both wet and dry. In fact, fly fishing is the only method permitted on the designated salmon rivers along the North Atlantic coast. Most anglers use 8- or 9-weight fly rods and traditional Atlantic salmon fly patterns (below).

Landlocks are commonly caught on small spoons fished on downriggers or lead-line outfits.

Black Rat

Silver Rat

Green Highlander

Black Dose

On bright days, use light-colored flies like the Green Highlander or Silver Rat; on dark days, dark flies like the Black Dose or Black Rat. Carry a selection of flies in sizes 6 to 2/0.

LAKE WHITEFISH

(Coregonis clupeaformis)

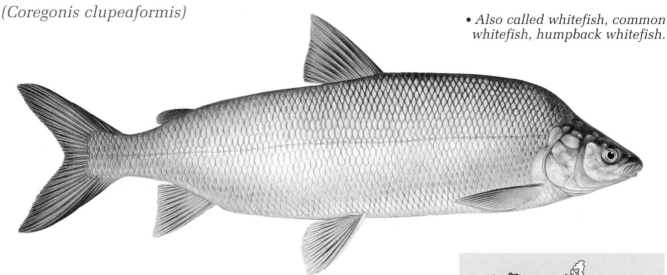

• *Also called whitefish, common whitefish, humpback whitefish.*

Lake whitefish have silvery sides with no markings and a greenish to brownish back. Like trout, char and salmon, they have an adipose fin. Lake whitefish resemble ciscoes (p. 150), but their mouth is much more underslung.

Lake whitefish range.

Varieties

Lake whitefish sometimes hybridize with inconnu and, in the Great Lakes, with ciscoes. Whitefish-cisco hybrids, sometimes called "mules," have a bright green hue, and their mouth is more underslung than that of a cisco but not as much as that of a whitefish.

Some lakes have a dwarf form of whitefish that becomes sexually mature at a length of only 5 or 6 inches.

Habitat

Because lake whitefish prefer water temperatures in the low 50s, they are found primarily in deep, cold, infertile lakes, often in the zone occupied by lake trout. They also inhabit shallower lakes in the Far North, where the water temperature stays cold all summer.

Feeding Habits

Lake whitefish feed mainly on small food items such as zooplankton, immature aquatic insects and tiny molluscs. But they sometimes take small fish. Although they are primarily bottom feeders, they also feed in midwater and sometimes take insects off the surface.

Spawning Behavior

In late fall, when the water temperature drops into the low 40s, lake whitefish move onto rocky, gravelly or sandy shoals to spawn. Some populations, however, spawn in rivers. The fish scatter their eggs at random in water less than 25 feet deep, usually at night. Sometimes spawners can be seen jumping and thrashing on the surface. After spawning, the parents abandon the eggs, which hatch in spring.

Age/Growth

Lake whitefish are long-lived, with a maximum life span of about 17 years in the southern part of their range and 28 years in the northern part. They commonly reach a weight of 4 to 6 pounds and have been known to grow much larger. In 1918, a 42-pounder was netted off Isle Royale in the Michigan waters of Lake Superior.

Dwarf lake whitefish, however, seldom reach a weight of more than ¼ pound.

World Record

15 pounds, 6 ounces; Clear Lake, Ontario; May 21, 1983.

Typical Growth Rate

Age	Length (inches)	Weight (pounds)
1	5.1	—
3	11.8	0.9
5	15.2	1.7
7	17.9	2.5
9	19.7	3.3
11	21.6	3.9
13	23.2	4.7
15	24.7	5.4
17	26.0	6.2

Fishing Facts

Lake whitefish have always been popular as a food fish. Although their flesh is quite oily, they are excellent when smoked, baked or boiled. Whitefish are seldom the main target of anglers, but they are gaining favor among fly fishermen because of their willingness to rise to a dry fly.

Look for whitefish dimpling the surface on calm mornings or evenings. It's not uncommon to see hundreds of fish sipping in midges or other tiny insects.

A slip-bobber rig and a small jig make a good combination for catching whitefish suspended in the mid-depths. Just find some fish with your depth finder and set the float accordingly.

CISCO

(Coregonus artedii)

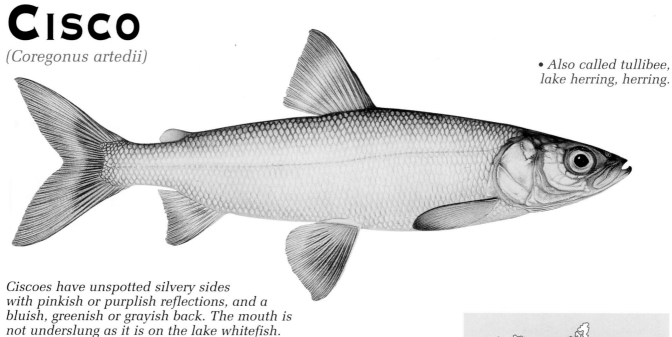

• *Also called tullibee,
lake herring, herring.*

*Ciscoes have unspotted silvery sides
with pinkish or purplish reflections, and a
bluish, greenish or grayish back. The mouth is
not underslung as it is on the lake whitefish.*

Varieties

Ciscoes sometimes hybridize with lake whitefish, round whitefish and other coregonids. They have also been known to cross with inconnu.

Like lake whitefish, ciscoes have a "dwarf" form that matures at a length of less than 6 inches. A deep-bodied form, called the "tullibee," is found in numerous lakes in the southern part of the range.

Habitat

Ciscoes are found in the same deep, cold, infertile lakes as lake whitefish. But they can tolerate slightly warmer water, so they also inhabit shallower, more fertile lakes whose depths are well-oxygenated. In the northern part of their range, they are sometimes found in large rivers. Their

preferred temperature range is 53 to 57°F.

Feeding Habits

The diet consists mainly of zooplankton, but ciscoes also feed on immature and adult insects, small crustaceans, small fish and fish eggs. Ciscoes feed on the bottom, on the surface or anywhere in between.

Spawning Behavior

Ciscoes spawn in late fall at water temperatures in the

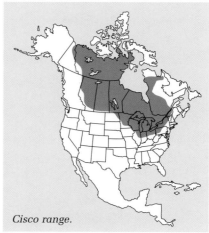

Cisco range.

upper 30s to low 40s. The eggs are scattered over most any kind of bottom and at a variety of depths ranging from less than 20 to more than 200 feet. The parents do

Tullibees have a considerably deeper body than ordinary ciscoes.

not guard the eggs, which hatch in spring.

Age/Growth

The maximum life span is about 12 years. Tullibees commonly reach a weight of 3 or 4 pounds; ordinary ciscoes seldom exceed 2.

World Record

7 pounds, 6 ounces; Cedar Lake, Manitoba; April 11, 1986.

Typical Growth Rate

Age	Length (inches)	Weight (pounds)
1	8.0	—
2	10.5	.4
3	12.5	.8
4	13.7	1.2
5	14.6	1.4
6	15.5	1.7
7	16.0	1.9
8	16.5	2.1

Fishing Facts

When the mayflies are hatching, you'll often see huge schools of ciscoes slurping them off the surface. That's the time to get out your fly rod and tie on a mayfly-imitating nymph or dry fly. Ice fishing for ciscoes (particularly tullibees) is becoming more popular on many northern lakes.

When ice fishing, look for suspended ciscoes on your depth finder. It's not unusual to find them 20 or more feet off the bottom. Active jigging usually works better than pausing between jig strokes.

Remove the hook from a jigging spoon and add a short length of mono and an ice fly tipped with a grub. The jigging spoon adds flash and provides the weight needed to get the bait down to the fish.

INCONNU

(Stenodus leucichthys)

• Also called sheefish, Arctic sheefish, conny, tarpon of the North.

Inconnu have silvery sides with no spots and a greenish to brownish back. The head is much broader than that of a whitefish or cisco, the mouth is much larger and the lower jaw projects well beyond the upper.

Varieties

There are two subspecies of of inconnu, or sheefish: *Stenodus leucichthys nelma*, found in Alaska, the Northwest Territories and Siberia; and *Stenodus leucichthys leucichthys*, found only in the Caspian Sea drainage.

Habitat

In coastal areas, sheefish are anadromous, but they are also found in deep, cold inland lakes such as Great Slave.

Feeding Habits

Adult sheefish feed almost exclusively on fish, including whitefish, northern pike and chinook salmon. They may even eat their own young.

Spawning Behavior

Sheefish in coastal rivers begin their upstream migration in spring. They some-times swim as much as 1,000 miles upstream and reach their spawning grounds in fall. Lake-dwelling sheefish migrate downstream in fall to spawn in outlet rivers. Spawning usually takes place at a water temperature of about 40°F. The fish scatter their eggs over a rubble bottom and make no attempt to protect them. An individual sheefish spawns only once every 2 to 4 years.

Age/Growth

The maximum life span is about 19 years. Inconnu grow much faster than other kinds of whitefish and commonly reach weights of 20 to 30 pounds.

World Record

53 pounds; Pah River, Alaska; August 20, 1986.

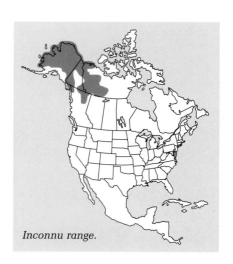

Inconnu range.

Typical Growth Rate

Age	Length (inches)	Weight (pounds)
1	5.4	—
3	13.8	0.9
5	19.5	2.9
7	25.8	7.4
9	30.9	10.6
11	34.5	13.0
13	37.6	16.1
15	41.1	21.5
17	44.3	27.4

Fishing Facts

The aerial antics of a hooked sheefish partially account for the name "tarpon of the North," but there's yet another reason: With their large, bony mouth and silvery flanks, sheefish vaguely resemble tarpon. Most sheefish are taken by casting with spoons and spinners, but they can also be caught on large, gaudy streamers.

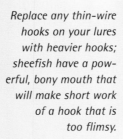

Look for sheefish in slow-moving water or eddies. You'll seldom find the fish holding in swift runs.

Replace any thin-wire hooks on your lures with heavier hooks; sheefish have a powerful, bony mouth that will make short work of a hook that is too flimsy.

ARCTIC GRAYLING

(Thymallus arcticus)

• *Also called American grayling, Arctic trout, tittimeg, sailfin.*

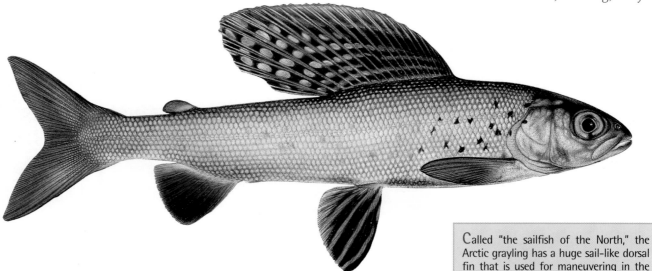

The grayling's distinctive dorsal fin has rows of bluish spots and its upper margin is tinged with white or pink. The sides are an iridescent purplish-gray, with scales much larger than those of other salmonids. The tail, pectoral and anal fins are usually yellowish and the pelvic fins have lengthwise stripes of black and pink. The male (above) has a long dorsal fin which, when folded down, extends almost to the adipose fin.

Called "the sailfish of the North," the Arctic grayling has a huge sail-like dorsal fin that is used for maneuvering in the swift current in which it normally lives.

Arctic grayling range.

Habitat

Grayling thrive in cold, clear streams and rivers, but they are also found in the shallow portions of deep, cold, infertile lakes. They prefer icy cold water (42 to 50°F) and a rocky bottom.

The largest grayling populations exist in the Northwest Territories, Alaska, British Columbia, Alberta, Manitoba and Saskatchewan. There are fishable populations in Montana, Wyoming, Utah and Idaho, mainly in high-elevation lakes.

Although grayling were once common in the Midwest, they were eliminated by fishing pressure and stream-habitat degradation. Efforts are currently being made to reintroduce the fish to some Midwestern waters.

Feeding Habits

Grayling prefer small food items such as insects, salmon eggs, crustaceans, clams and snails. In streams, grayling do most of their feeding in shallow riffle areas. In lakes, you'll see them dimpling

Female grayling have a much shorter dorsal fin than males. When folded down, it falls well short of the adipose fin.

around inlets and outlets or near downed trees and overhanging brush along the shoreline.

Spawning Behavior

In early spring, grayling move into small tributary streams to spawn, usually when the water temperature reaches the mid to upper 40s. Unlike other salmonids, they do not dig redds, but deposit their eggs directly onto a gravelly or rocky bottom.

Age/Growth

Because grayling grow slowly and have a relatively short life span (usually 6 years or less), they seldom reach a weight of more than 4 pounds. In the western states, they rarely exceed 1 pound.

World Record

5 pounds, 15 ounces; Katseyedie River, Northwest Territories; August 16, 1967.

Typical Growth Rate

Age	Length (inches)	Weight (pounds)
1	6.2	—
2	8.8	0.2
3	10.5	0.4
4	12.4	0.6
5	14.2	1.0
6	15.5	1.2
7	16.6	1.5
8	17.4	1.8
9	18.0	2.0

Fishing Facts

Perhaps the most surface-oriented feeder of all the salmonids, grayling are willing biters, especially when they're feeding in riffles. They will give you a good tussle on light tackle, frequently jumping when first hooked.

Because grayling prefer such small food items, anglers use very small lures and baits, including tiny spinners, spoons and flies as well as salmon eggs, worms, maggots, grasshoppers and just about any other small bait used for stream trout.

The ease with which grayling can be caught makes it difficult for fisheries managers to maintain decent populations. In easily accessible waters, it's important to practice catch-and-release.

Look for grayling in riffle areas with plenty of good-sized rocks that provide current breaks for fish.

When grayling are dimpling the surface, try a dark-colored dry fly in a size 14 or smaller. When there is no surface activity, use a small nymph.

INDEX

S

Sailfin. *See* Arctic grayling
Salmon, 39, 105. *See also* Atlantic
    salmon; Chinook salmon; Chum
    salmon; Coho salmon; Pink
    salmon; Sockeye salmon
Salmon eggs, 129, 143, 155
Sand bass. *See* White bass
Sand pike. *See* Sauger
Sardins, 101
Sauger, 39, 44–45
    age/growth, 44
    feeding habits, 44
    fishing facts, 45
    habitat, 44
    spawning behavior, 44
    varieties, 44
    world record, 45
Saugeyes, 45
Sea perch. *See* White perch
Sebago salmon. *See* Atlantic salmon
Shad, 42, 87
Shad dart for American shad, 103
Shadow bass, 34
Sheefish. *See* Inconnu
Shellcracker. *See* Redear sunfish
Shoal bass, 14, 15
Shovelhead cat. *See* Flathead catfish
Shovelnose cat. *See* Paddlefish
Shrimp, 27, 97, 137
Silver bass. *See* White bass; White
    crappie
Silver cat. *See* Blue catfish
Silver char. *See* Arctic char
Silver perch. *See* White perch
Silver pike, 51
Silver salmon. *See* Coho salmon
Siscowet, 123
Skamania rainbow trout, 108
Skipjack herring, 101
Slip-bobber rig for bluegills, 23
Slip-sinker rig, 71, 97
Smallmouth bass, 10–11
    age/growth, 10
    feeding habits, 10
    fishing facts, 11
    habitat, 10
    spawning behavior, 10
    varieties, 10
    world record, 11
Smelt, 42, 125
Snagging rig for paddlefish, 99
Snake. *See* Northern pike
Soap for black bullheads, 75
Sockeye salmon, 141–43
    age/growth, 141
    feeding habits, 141
    fishing facts, 142–43
    habitat, 141
    spawning behavior, 141
    varieties, 141
    world record, 141
Southern brown bullhead, 76
Spawn bags for coho salmon, 137
Speck. *See* Black crappie; White
    perch
Speckled perch. *See* Black crappie;
    White crappie
Speckled trout. *See* Brook trout
Spinnerbaits, 9, 11, 13, 23, 57
Spinners, 15, 17, 25, 29, 31, 43, 47,
    53, 59, 65, 89, 91, 109, 113, 129,
    135, 137, 139, 153, 155
Spin-n-Glo for chinook salmon, 135
Spin-rig for white crappies, 19

Splake, 120, 123, 124
Sponge bugs, 23, 31
Spoonbill cat. *See* Paddlefish
Spoons, 53, 59, 65, 89, 91, 109, 113,
    125, 129, 131, 135, 137, 147, 151,
    153, 155
Spot bass. *See* Spotted bass
Spotfin pike. *See* Sauger
Spotted bass, 12–13
    age/growth, 13
    feeding habits, 12
    fishing facts, 13
    habitat, 12
    spawning behavior, 12
    varieties, 12
    world record, 13
Spotted cat. *See* Channel catfish
Squaretail. *See* Brook trout
Steelhead, 108, 109
Stickbaits for muskellunge, 57
Stinger hook for saugers, 45
Stinkbaits, 65, 75, 77
Streaker. *See* Yellow bass
Streamers, 59, 91, 113, 129, 131
Striped bass, 81, 85–87
    age/growth, 86
    feeding habits, 85
    fishing facts, 87
    habitat, 85
    spawning behavior, 86
    varieties, 85
    world record, 86
Striper. *See* Striped bass; White bass;
    Yellow bass
Stumpknocker. *See* Redear sunfish;
    Warmouth
Sturgeon. *See* Lake sturgeon; White
    sturgeon
Sturgeon family, 93–97
Suckers for flathead catfish, 67
Sunapee trout. *See* Arctic char
Sunfish, 5, 39. *See also* Green sun-
    fish; Longear sunfish; Redbreast
    sunfish; Redear sunfish
Sunfish family, 5–38
Sun perch. See bluegill

T

Tailspin for spotted bass, 13
Tarpon of the North. *See* Inconnu
Temperate bass family, 81–99
Texas-rig for largemouth bass, 9
Threadfin shad, 101
Tiger muskie, 51, 55
Tiger trout, 111, 120
Tittimeg. *See* Arctic grayling
Togue. See Lake trout
Topwaters, 9, 11, 57, 59
Trolling plugs for chinook salmon,
    135
Trotlining
    for blue catfish, 71
    for flathead catfish, 67
Trout, 39. *See also* Brook trout;
    Brown trout; Bull trout; Cutthroat
    trout; Dolly Varden; Golden trout;
    Lake trout; Rainbow trout
Trout family, 105–55
True bass, 81
Tullibee, 150. *See also* Cisco
Twist-on leader wrap, for rainbow
    trout, 109
Tyee. *See* Chinook salmon

V

Volcano Creek golden trout, 118

W

Walleye, 39, 41–43
    age/growth, 41–42
    feeding habits, 41
    fishing facts, 43
    habitat, 41
    spawning behavior, 41
    varieties, 41
    world record, 42
Walleyed pike. *See* Walleye
Warmouth, 24, 36–37
    age/growth, 36
    feeding habits, 36
    fishing facts, 37
    habitat, 36
    spawning behavior, 36
    varieties, 36
    world record, 36
Waxworms for yellow perch, 47
Weedless spoons for chain pickerel,
    59
West Slope cutthroat trout, 117
Wet flies. *See also* Flies, 17, 25, 29,
    31, 37, 91, 147
White bass, 81, 82–83
    age/growth, 82
    feeding habits, 82
    fishing facts, 83
    habitat, 82
    spawning behavior, 82
    varieties, 82
    world record, 82
White catfish, 72–73
    age/growth, 72–73
    feeding habits, 72
    fishing facts, 73
    habitat, 72
    spawning behavior, 72
    world record, 73
White crappie, 18–19
    age/growth, 18
    feeding habits, 18
    fishing facts, 19
    habitat, 18
    spawning behavior, 18
    varieties, 18
    world record, 18
Whitefish, 105. *See also* Lake white-
    fish
White perch, 81, 90–91
    age/growth, 90
    feeding habits, 90
    fishing facts, 91
    habitat, 90
    spawning behavior, 90
    varieties, 90
    world record, 90
White shad. *See* American shad
White sturgeon, 96–97
    age/growth, 96
    feeding habits, 96
    fishing facts, 97
    habitat, 96
    spawning behavior, 96
    world record, 96
White-whiskered bullhead. *See*
    Yellow bullhead
Wipers. *See* Striped bass; White bass
Wire leaders for chain pickerel, 59
Worms, 15, 23, 25, 27, 29, 47, 65, 75,
    109, 143, 155

Y

Yarn fly for cutthroat trout, 116
Yellow bass, 81, 88–89
    age/growth, 89
    feeding habits, 88
    fishing facts, 89
    habitat, 88
    spawning behavior, 88–89
    varieties, 88
    world record, 89
Yellowbelly bullhead. *See* Black bull-
    head
Yellowbelly sunfish. *See* Redbreast
    sunfish
Yellow bullhead, 78–79
    age/growth, 79
    feeding habits, 78
    fishing facts, 79
    habitat, 78
    spawning behavior, 78-79
    world record, 79
Yellow cat. *See* Flathead catfish;
    Yellow bullhead
Yellow perch, 39, 46–47
    age/growth, 46–47
    feeding habits, 46
    fishing facts, 47
    habitat, 46
    spawning behavior, 46
    world record, 47
Yellowstone cutthroat trout, 115
Yellow sunfish. *See* Pumpkinseed